IT'S A WHOLE NEW BALLGAME

HOW SOCIAL MEDIA IS CHANGING SPORTS

THE HAMPTON PRESS COMMUNICATION SERIES
Mass Communication and Journalism
Lee B. Becker, supervisory editor

Critical Conversations: A Theory of Press Accountability
Wendy Wyatt Barger
China's Window on the World: TV News, Social Knowledge,
and International Spectacles
Tsan-Kuo Chang with *Jian Wang & Yanru Chen*
History and Future of Mass Media: An Integrated Perspective
David Demers
Heroes in a Global World
Susan J. Drucker & Gary Gumpert (eds.)
The Evolution of Key Mass Communication Concepts: Honoring Jack M.
McLeod
Sharon Dunwoody, Lee B. Becker,
Douglas M. McLeod & Gerald M. Kiosicki (eds.)
Ethics & Evil in the Public Sphere: Media, Universal Values & Global
Development: Essays in honor of Clifford G. Christians
Robert Fortner & Mark Fackler (Eds.)
Journalism Education in Europe and North America:
An International Comparison
Romy Fröhlich & Christina Holtz-Bacha (eds.)
Women Journalists in the Western World: What Surveys Tell Us
Romy Fröhlich & Sue A. Lafky
Communication and Terrorism: Public and Media Responses to 9/11
Bradley S. Greenberg (ed.)
Views from the Fairway: Media Explorations of Identity in Golf
Heather L. Hundley & Andrew C. Billings
Arab Journalists in Transnational Media
Noha Mellor
The Gendered Newsroom: How Journalists Experience the Changing World
of Media
Louise North
Tilted Mirrors: Media Alignment with Political and Social Change—
A Community Structure Approach
John C. Pollack
Sourcing the News: Key Issues in Journalism—An Innovative Study
of the Israeli Press
Zvi Reich
It's a Whole New Ballgame: How Social Media is Changing Sports
Jimmy Sanderson
Journalism And Meaning-Making: Reading the Newspaper
Verica Rupar (ed.)

IT'S A WHOLE NEW BALLGAME

HOW SOCIAL MEDIA IS CHANGING SPORTS

Jimmy Sanderson

Arizona State University

HAMPTON PRESS, INC.
NEW YORK, NEW YORK

Printed in the United States of America

Library of Congress Cataloging-in-Publication Data

Sanderson, Jimmy.
   It's a whole new ballgame : how social media is changing sports / Jimmy Sanderson.
        p. cm. -- (The Hampton Press Communication series (Mass Media and Journalism subseries))
   Includes bibliographical references and index.
   ISBN 978-1-61289-052-4 (hardbound) -- ISBN 978-1-61289-053-1 (paperbound)
   1. Mass media and sports. 2. Social media. 3. Communication in sports. 4. Sports-
-Social aspects. I. Title.
   GV742.S26 2011
   070.449796--dc23
                           2011033749

Hampton Press, Inc.
307 Seventh Avenue
New York, NY 10001

CONTENTS

PREFACE

I have fond memories of the 1986 NFL Draft. I was 9 years old, in the third grade, and remember copiously reading the lengthy list of drafted players in *The Arizona Republic*. I was so intrigued by this process that I wanted to have my "own" record of the Draft. To accomplish this goal, I transcribed the entire 12 rounds of Draft results from the newspaper using my family's electronic typewriter. I proudly delivered my finished report to my third-grade teacher, and although she probably wondered what I was doing, she showered me with praise and mentioned my achievement in front of the class. As the years progressed, I began making my own "mock" drafts in numerous paper binders, diligently recording how I believed the Draft would unfold. As I entered junior high and high school I derived some social capital by coming to school the Monday after the Draft and inform-ing my friends about who had been added to their favorite team.

As I was writing this book, I reflected on that experience and chuckled at how primitive those efforts now look in contemporary society. I am amazed at the volume of Internet sites, including blogs, where people pro-mote their NFL Draft prognostications. In some cases, the traffic on these sites is sufficient enough to allow site creators to sell advertising. Perhaps if these capabilities had existed when I was growing up, I could have earned money through my Draft predictions instead of delivering newspapers! More than two decades have passed since I first bonded with the NFL Draft experience, and I highly doubt such a process would repeat itself today. The NFL Draft is now a spectacular television production, and results are streamed immediately via television and the Internet, making it unnecessary to wait for the newspaper.

Nevertheless, I am confident that similar narratives are shared by a multitude of sports fans across the world. The affection that sports fans feel toward their favorite players and teams has exponentially magnified through the introduction and proliferation of social media sites. For sports fans, these domains enhance perceptions that athletes and sports figures are "closer" to us, and the interactive possibilities offered by these sites are both fascinating and troublesome. It is remarkable to consider how quickly social media has permeated across and become embedded in the sports world. Although these technologies have increased fan–athlete interaction, they also have generated no shortage of controversy. Indeed, it seems that hardly a day goes by without a newswire running a story about content on an athlete's or a sports figure's social media site.

Accordingly, athletes, sports organizations, and sports practitioners are grappling with a multitude of questions as they attempt to harness the power of social media. The need to provide discussion areas for the role of social media in sports is the driving force behind this book. However, with the consistent supply of stories about the social media use of athletes and sports figures, it was particularly challenging to determine which examples to include and which to leave out. Thus, as there is so much happening with this topic, there are a number of directions that offer exciting opportunities for future work. I love sports and writing this book has been a tremendous pleasure. I hope that others enjoy reading this book as much as I enjoyed writing it.

Finally, any book is the product of a number of individuals, well beyond the person's name that appears underneath the title. To that end, I would be remiss if I did not take the opportunity to express my gratitude to several people. First, I would like to thank Barbara Bernstein and Dr. Lee Becker for their kindness and professionalism throughout this process. I am particularly indebted to Dr. Becker for giving me the opportunity to write this book and for his helpful comments throughout the revision process; they greatly strengthened the final product. Next, I am immensely indebted to Dr. Jeffrey W. Kassing, my mentor, for bringing me into the fascinating world of sports communication scholarship. I still remember 3 years ago when he called me down to his office and asked me if I wanted to participate in a project about Floyd Landis and parasocial interaction. Through that one gesture, I have experienced more benefits than I could have ever imagined will be forever grateful for having such a wonderful and approachable mentor along with a great friend. Whatever scholarly achievements I experience will be intricately linked with his guidance and encouragement. I could not have asked for a better mentor.

I am also grateful to Vicki Sebade for reading the manuscript and offering valuable input that greatly improved the final product. Thanks for being such a wonderful friend and for being so enthusiastic about this project. Last, but certainly not least, I am very grateful for my wife Kirsten, and my two boys, Walker and Connor, for their patience with me as I worked on this project. Although it took me away from doing things with them, their support was constant. I am very fortunate to have such an understanding and wonderful family. I am amazed at the love they give me, and even though I fall short in so many ways, they continue to tolerate me and unconditionally love me, for which I am eternally thankful.

FOREWORD

In summer 2006 I was captivated, as were many fans of cycling, by the dramatic victory of Floyd Landis in the Tour de France. Lance Armstrong had retired the previous year—for the first time—and the sport was looking for its next champion. Few expected it to be an American, much less one who had previously ridden in support of Armstrong. Yet that year Landis won the tour in dramatic fashion, losing the leader's yellow jersey after a miserable day on the bike only to recapture that time predominantly in one epic breakaway ride across five mountain passes. No one—fans, managers, riders—expected him to stay away that day and to come back into overall contention. But he did and his victory quickly became the stuff of legend. But in the end it proved short-lived and too good to be true. Soon after the tour finished news broke that Landis had tested positive for using performance-enhancing drugs. He spent the next year fighting the allegations, appealing to the highest level of arbitration. His efforts were unsuccessful and eventually he was stripped of his title and banned from the sport for 2 years. He maintained his innocence throughout.

Landis' dramatic victory and the subsequent fight to clear his name provided an intriguing opportunity to observe and explore how fans were reacting to a rising, fighting, and free-falling athlete. To understand this phenomenon from the perspective of fans I simply had to look to the countless messages people had posted on his Web site. Here was a cornucopia of fan sentiment. What were these people trying to achieve? What did they hope to convey? These were the questions I was pondering when Jimmy Sanderson stopped by my office. I shared the idea of studying this body of texts with him. A line of inquiry and a long-standing research partnership were born. At the time neither of us was all that familiar with social media, but we both saw the potential impact it was beginning to have on sport. That impact has only gained in momentum and complexity. And this book clearly illustrates how social media have shaped communication and sport.

It is difficult to keep one's finger on the pulse of social media and sports, as this is an ever-changing landscape—one that shifts daily, sometimes seismically. But that is what Jimmy Sanderson has managed to do in this work. Granted the connection between the two will continue to evolve and develop, but over time his text will stand as an early and important testament to how social media and sport intersect. As he notes, social media have only been around for a handful of years. Yet he has been working at the forefront in this area that entire time. This book is a demonstration of the close eye he has kept on developing trends in social media and sport. He explains these trends in clear terms and provides abundant examples to develop each. As a result this book strikes a nice balance. It manages to be focused and comprehensive. It is scholarly and theoretical, yet remains accessible and prescriptive. Scholars, students, and practitioners alike would benefit from reading it.

Landis was back in the news in summer 2010 when he admitted to doping during his cycling career. Reportedly, he came forward because he wants to see the sport cleaned up. His admission also implicated a host of other high-profile riders including Armstrong. At the moment, those allegations are under investigation. But people already have reacted in force via social media, with some celebrating Landis for finally coming clean and others vilifying him for misleading fans and sullying fellow cyclists' reputations. Like the sport of professional cycling, the increasingly powerful bond between social media and sport will continue to roll on. This book will mark the starting point for our understanding of that bond and how it plays out.

Jeffrey W. Kassing,
Arizona State University

INTRODUCTION

I regularly listen to sports talk radio as I drive in my car. One afternoon as I was driving home, my ears perked up when I heard one of the local hosts mention what has become an increasingly relevant sports topic—Twitter. The hosts then discussed a tweet (a "tweet" is the popular term for one's Twitter posts) sent by Phoenix Coyotes player Paul Bissonnette, commenting on the National Hockey League's (NHL) rejection of a contract signed by free-agent player Ilya Kovalchuk:

> kovalchuck's gana have to give lap dances for 20 years instead of getting them now that he got rejected. sory communist. back to the soviet.

Although Bissonnette quickly apologized for his comment, his Twitter account was deleted within 1 hour after this posting (Wyshynski, 2010). Bissonette's Twitter account eventually returned, but incidents of this nature have become consistent sports media topics. Although most of the content posted by these individuals is mundane, some messages have generated significant media attention and public relations dilemmas. These issues are growing more prevalent and newsworthy, necessitating athletes, sports organizations, and other vested parties (e.g., agents, players associations) to be assertive in developing collaborative solutions to harness the power of social media—*and social media is very powerful.*

Through social media, athletes and sports figures have intriguing broadcast capabilities that are changing the ways that sports media is produced and consumed. Fans are capitalizing on the interactivity offered by social media channels to directly engage athletes and sports organization personnel. These connective capabilities promote and foster closeness and identification for fans with athletes and sports figures.[1] In writing this book, I bring attention to some of the more pressing issues that social media creates for athletes and sports organizations. Additionally, I hope to encourage sports organizations, athletes, and other interested groups to manage social media strategically and collaboratively. It only takes one social media posting to generate significant controversy, an outcome to which many athletes and sports organizations can attest. However, social media offers many positive benefits for athletes and sports organization as well. In maximizing these advantages and strategically working to minimize social media miscues, the social media environment in sports, currently marked by uncertainty and conflict, will become more defined and harmonious. It will be interesting to observe the interplay between sports and social media as time goes on. In my estimation, research will be a key factor that will greatly contribute to optimal social media programs in the sports world.

Accordingly, I offer a short rationale for using sports as a context to study social media. It is difficult to find an avenue in life that is not influenced or affected to some degree, by sports. Sports hold a prominent place in society, and in many cases, represents wider societal and cultural trends and discourses (Reid, 2010; Rowe & Gilmour, 2009; Wenner, 2007). People are highly invested in sports and as a result, fandom is an important social identity component. Additionally, children are socialized into sports at very young ages, and sports media has exponentially multiplied and is now available on demand from numerous outlets. These areas (and many others) all are significantly influenced by communication. Yet sports communication scholars have faced an uphill battle in bringing legitimacy to the study of this area, although acceptance from the scholarly community is increasing (Kassing, 2009b; Krizek, 2008). Exciting research is being conducted in sports communication and there is no shortage of research topics, particularly with the advent of social media.

This book represents one direction in sports communication research. The purpose of this book is to explore how social media is affecting sports, and in chronicling these changes, positioning sport as a prominent site that can greatly inform us about media practices and interpersonal, organizational, and mass communication. To that end, I hope that this work will contribute to the growing body of sports communication research and become a valuable tool for communication and media scholars.

---

[1]Readers will note misspelling and grammatical errors in the tweets used as examples in this text. This is intentional. The tweets were left intact. Interestingly, Jim DeLorenzo, vice president of the sports marketing agency Octagon Digital, and founder of Twackle.com, noted that misspelling and grammatical errors increase identification. As people often have misspellings and improper grammar in their text messages, seeing the same trends in postings by athletes and sports figures resonates with their fans (Lemke, 2009).

1

LAYING THE GROUNDWORK

There was perhaps no bigger sports story in 2010 than the free agency of National Basketball Association (NBA) superstar LeBron James. This story reached its dramatic conclusion on July 8, 2010, when James publicly revealed that he would leave the Cleveland Cavaliers and join the Miami Heat. Prior to this announcement, there was intense speculation about James' ultimate destination, which extended well beyond the sports media universe. Given this prominent coverage, it was not surprising that James disclosed his intentions in an unprecedented manner. James announced his decision to play for the Heat during a 1-hour interview titled "The Decision," with sports reporter Jim Gray, broadcast via ESPN and staged at a Connecticut Boys and Girls Club. The program drew nearly 10 million viewers, becoming the third most-watched program on cable television to that point in the year, trailing only the National Football League's (NFL) Pro Bowl, and an ICarly episode on Nickelodeon (ESPN.com, 2010c). As groundbreaking as this event was, a significant precursor to "The Decision" occurred on July 6, 2010, when James opened a Twitter account.

In response, people flocked to Twitter to "follow" James (a feature that allows Twitter users to receive status updates from other users and reply to and retransmit these messages on their Twitter account). Indeed, less than an hour after James' profile appeared, and before he had even authored a single posting, he had nearly 18,000 followers (Withers, 2010). On the morning of his announcement, James fueled anticipation for the event by posting on Twitter that people could use the site to send him questions about his decision—an invitation that prompted numerous questions from audience members. Although it was impractical for James to answer every question that was posted, the immense participation this request created vividly demonstrated an important outcome that social media has produced in the sports world. Namely, social media allows athletes to be more directly involved in media production processes. Additionally, social media enables athletes to integrate fans into their media messages, a capability that brings fans closer to athletes. This connection is but one implication that has emerged through the rapid proliferation of communication technology.

In the current digital era, media consumers have a plethora of options available to them. Indeed, there is so much information that is electronically available that searching for and obtaining information online can be daunting. The Internet has ushered in a multitude of communicative possibilities that only a few years ago seemed difficult to imagine. It was not all that long ago that people handwrote letters, located information in phone books, and used maps to obtain directions. Although these practices have not entirely disappeared, digital resources clearly have transformed them. In addition to the electronic retrieval of information, people are able to communicate and interact with others worldwide, overcoming geographical and spatial barriers.

Such capabilities have only been magnified through the emergence of social media sites. These sites, by their nature, allow the creation and wide transmission of content that fuels interaction, collaboration, and community. These possibilities were available during the early days of the Internet (more commonly known as Web 1.0), however, many operating systems were not equipped to handle the file-sharing capacities so readily available in the computers and mobile devices of today. Additionally, participation in many of these electronic forums was primarily one way. Although interactive communication did occur in chat rooms and via instant messaging programs, most Web sites had minimal utility for communicative exchanges.

The communication and interaction occurring through what has popularly been termed "Web 2.0," is remarkably demonstrated by social media. Scholars have suggested that Web 2.0 sites are "driven by social connections and user participation" (Song, 2010, p. 249), and have created a new Internet generation characterized by digital content creation and interactivity (Deuze, 2006). Social media offers people accessible sites where they can connect with others, create and share content, and more actively participate in media production and consumption. Accordingly, these sites have quickly gained millions of users. Consider Facebook, arguably the most popular social media site at the present time. Facebook currently has more than 500 million active users, 50% of whom use Facebook on any given day, and who spend 700 billion minutes per month accessing the site (Facebook.com, 2010).

Social media are inherently designed to facilitate connections. Social media have been conceptualized as "media that is architected by design to readily support participation, peer-to-peer conversation, collaboration and community" (Meraz, 2009, p. 682). Social media also

> refers to activities, practices, and behaviors among communities of people who gather online to share information, knowledge, and opinions using conversational media. . . . Web-based applications that make it possible to create and easily transmit content in the form of words, pictures, videos, and audios. (Safko & Brake, 2009, p. 6)

There are many factors that share responsibility for driving social media's popularity. However, the ability to create and distribute content is one of the more influential advantages that have contributed to the rise of social media. Social media requires minimal start-up costs, and although one's audience size varies, one only needs computer access or a mobile telephone to broadcast one's thoughts for public consumption. Thus, social media enables people to become active, rather than passive, media consumers. Accordingly, independent news-oriented blogs and Web sites that offer the public alternative options for media consumption have grown more prominent (Atton, 2009; Wall, 2005; C. Young, 2005).

Social media has become so embedded in the fabric of everyday life that it is impossible to cover every possible area, sector, or avenue, in which they have produced change. This text explores the impact of social media on the area of sports. In some respects, it is difficult to imagine another industry that has been so dramatically altered by social media as the sports world. Social media allows athletes to become more accessible to fans, a feature that has driven large audiences to athletes' social media sites. Additionally, athletes are capitalizing on social media to become more active media producers, an outcome that has both compelling and troubling implications. As a result, social media is becoming an increasingly popular sports topic, and examples are in large supply. The following accounts represent only a fraction of the stories that have surfaced as a result of social media use:

On March 23, 2009, Boston Red Sox pitcher Curt Schilling announced his retirement from professional baseball. Traditionally, an athlete's retirement announcement is a festive event, well attended by sports journalists and well constructed by the sports organization for which the athlete plays.

However, on this particular occasion, there was no elaborate press conference at historic Fenway Park; instead notification of Schilling's retirement
appeared on his blog—38pitches.com. Schilling posted a rather nondescript,
1,261-word blog posting entitled, "Calling it quits." There was no celebra-
tory press conference, no pomp and circumstance, merely a blog posting in
which Schilling, acting independently, succinctly summarized his career
and offered rationale for his decision to retire.

On April 11, 2009, Taylor Moseley, a freshman at North Carolina State
University, received a "cease-and-desist" letter from Michelle Lee, the university's athletic department compliance representative. The reason for the
letter? Moseley had created a Facebook group encouraging John Wall, the
top high school basketball player in the country, to attend North Carolina
State. This letter came in response to the National Collegiate Athletic
Association (NCAA) becoming aware of the group. NCAA spokesman
Erik Christianson commented that academic institutions needed to contact
creators of groups similar to Moseley's to educate them that these sites
potentially violate recruiting rules (Associated Press, 2009b). Moseley subsequently changed the name of his Facebook group from "John Wall
PLEASE come to NC STATE!!!!" to "Bring a National Title back to NC
STATE!" However, there were several other Facebook groups created that
encouraged Wall to attend other universities and Facebook groups of this
nature continue to appear.

On June 16, 2009, Minnesota Timberwolves player Kevin Love posted
on his Twitter account that head coach Kevin McHale had just been fired
by the organization. Although this was perhaps welcome news for fans of
the struggling franchise, there was one problem with Love's social media
declaration—the Timberwolves were not ready for this news to be
announced publicly. Naturally, the organization was barraged with a flurry
of questions regarding its decision. Such a response is hardly surprising,
considering that many sports journalists follow athletes on Twitter. This
incident demonstrates how social media reduces the ability of sports organizations to control information, and suggests that they must account for
the possibility that athletes will broadcast confidential information via
social media. Further complicating this issue, is that once an athlete has
broadcast the message, a record exists that makes it difficult for the athlete
or sports organization to attribute the message to media misinterpretation.

For instance, when athletes are interviewed face to face and divulge
confidential information, sports journalists can allow athletes the opportunity to clarify their remarks. If a favorable relationship exists, the reporter
may withhold disclosing the information until the sports organization has
publicly released the news. Although athletes can delete these messages
from their profiles, this does not prevent others from copying and distributing them across the Internet. Once information is released, it only takes a
moment before it quickly spreads, giving sports organizations little time to

prepare a sufficient public response. Interestingly, Love no longer has a Twitter account.

On September 28, 2009, head Texas Tech football coach Mike Leach banned players from using Twitter and Facebook. Leach implemented this policy after linebacker Marlon Williams posted a tweet asking why he was wasting his time sitting in a meeting, waiting for Leach, who was tardy. Additionally, after a loss to the University of Houston, offensive lineman Brandon Carter used Twitter to convey his frustrations that the team's current performance was incongruent with preseason expectations. In explaining this policy, Leach referred to Twitter and Facebook as "stupid distractions" (Associated Press, 2009g). Certainly, an argument can be made that Leach was acting within acceptable parameters by banning these social media sites (similar steps have been taken by the University of Miami and Boise State football programs).

However, social media offer athletes viable communication tools to expose issues with sports teams that could be indicators of bigger problems. This is particularly relevant in Leach's case, as he was terminated on December 31, 2009, for allegedly mistreating Adam James, an injured Texas Tech player. Leach and Texas Tech have been involved in a bitter court battle over his termination, and the extent to which James was mistreated has not been proven. Yet, it is worth noting that players were using social media to express frustration with Leach's leadership. Thus, the social media messages that Leach considered to be "stupid," may have in fact, been outlets for players to express concern about the manner in which he was directing the football program.

In March 2010, news reports surfaced indicating that Pittsburgh Steelers wide receiver Santonio Holmes had been accused of assaulting a woman in a Florida nightclub. Some fans were apparently upset by these reports and began directing criticism to Holmes for his alleged actions — via his Twitter account. On March 29, 2010, Holmes seemed to have had enough of these messages and tweeted to a fan, "y u tryna make me look like the bad guy. U shud try finding the worst thing that you could drink n kill urself." This message further exacerbated Holmes' volatile situation with the Steelers and the NFL (he was suspended for the first four games of the 2010-2011 season for violating the league's substance abuse policy) and on April 11, 2010, Holmes was traded to the New York Jets.

Considering the frequency with which stories involving athletes and social media are occurring, the time is right to explore how these communication tools are changing sports. In writing this book, I am attending to only *some* of the issues relating to sports and social media. The primary focus of this text is athletes, largely professional, but some amateur, and this work is largely centered on athletes in major American sports such as football, basketball, and baseball (although other sporting arenas will be used). In doing so, I fully recognize that there are a multitude of areas that warrant further discussion. I readily acknowledge this limitation and hope that others will build on this subject and eagerly explore additional intersections between sports and social media.

There also exist a multitude of social media channels that could be incorporated into an analysis of social media's influence on sports. Acknowledging this to be the case, this text centers primarily on blogs and Twitter — the current social media "of choice" for athletes. To a lesser extent, Facebook and discussion forums will be covered, particularly as it relates to fans creating content and voicing both support and contempt for athletes and sports personalities. Although these social media sites are currently among the most popular, interests and preferences are likely to change in the future. It will be crucial for sports organizations and scholars to address these emerging social media sites and their accompanying effects on sports. I firmly believe that there will be no shortage of work to be done in this area, especially applied research — scholarship that both athletes and sports organizations can employ to strategically manage social media and mitigate public relations issues. Thus, athletes, sports organizations, players associations, sports leagues, collegiate athletic programs, and other vested parties must actively monitor social media trends and work in concert to manage these communicative tools.

In addition to this introductory chapter and a concluding chapter, the text is segmented into three chapters, each of which details a sports area that has been affected by social media. These areas are sports media, sports organizations, and athlete–fan communication. A brief preview of each chapter is now provided.

SOCIAL MEDIA AND SPORTS MEDIA

Social media have dramatically altered mass media production and consumption. Audience members are now able to produce and broadcast information, a task for which various social media channels can be used. Accordingly, scholars have observed an emerging trend of "amateur" or "citizen" journalism, wherein members of the general public offer alternative viewpoints and commentary via the Internet (Carpenter, 2008; Hamdy, 2009; Witt, 2004). With the vast number of people now providing news updates and commentary online, it is becoming more complex to distinguish who actually is a "journalist" ("Who is a Journalist?," 2008). This increasing competition has required mass media organizations to incorporate blogging and other social media formats into their news-delivery systems (Butler & Sagas, 2008).

These trends also have filtered into sports media. Whereas in the past the sports media hierarchy was quite rigid, sports media consumers now have a number of choices available when seeking to obtain information. Sports media scholars Brett Hutchins and David Rowe (2009) suggested that this flattening of the sports media hierarchy constitutes a "digital plentitude" for sports media consumers. In this landscape, sports media audiences now have a vast array of choices to select from when consuming sports information. Sports organizations and sports leagues are taking advantage of this trend, and are supplementing their television broadcasting resources with social media tools—particularly Facebook and Twitter. One notable example of this trend was the 2010 Winter Olympics in Vancouver, British Columbia. For the first time, the International Olympic Committee (IOC) designated a "head of social media," Alex Huot, who predicted that the Vancouver Olympiad would become the "first social media Olympics" (van Hemert, 2010).

Just as mass media organizations and sports leagues are capitalizing on social media platforms, athletes also are entering this competitive media market. They routinely are using social media, particularly Twitter, to break news and provide commentary on both sports and political stories. To what extent these public announcements constitute "journalism" remains to be seen. Certainly, it would be difficult to consider mundane commentary as "journalism," but there may be occasions when social media content may reflect journalistic functions. For example, the critical commentary that Texas Tech athletes posted about Mike Leach could be a form of investigatory journalism. Indeed, in situations where a coach is engaging in misconduct, who is in a better position than players to report such behavior?

Moreover, social media have introduced significant changes in the relationship between athletes and sports reporters. Social media use by athletes is certainly influencing sports journalists, who must consistently follow athletes' social media commentary to obtain news that they can then "break" on their organization's Web site. Additionally, many of these reporters also maintain their own social media presence (primarily on Twitter) in an effort to remain competitive for the attention of the sports media consumer. With the ability for fans to connect directly with athletes via social media, and to be immediately notified when new content has been posted, it will be interesting to see if fans become less reliant on sports reporters for information.

Athletes also are frequently subjected to "framing" by sports journalists. In other words, their actions and comments are packaged in news stories in ways that shape interpretation by audience members. In the past, athletes who felt they were inaccurately portrayed in the media could perhaps share these feelings with sympathetic reporters or team personnel; yet, these efforts were limited in their scope. With social media, however, athletes now have accessible forums that enable them to counter perceived negative representations by sports reporters to wide audiences.

Furthermore, with the ability of fans to comment on these postings, athletes can use this participation to gauge public support for their refutations of perceived biases in sports news stories.

Thus, as athletes become more assertive in releasing sports information and countering perceived inaccuracies in press portrayals, sports reporters become less involved in filtering that information. As fans turn to athletes rather than reporters for sports information, conflict between athletes and sports journalists has resulted. It will be interesting to observe which of these groups fans offer support to, and the extent to which an athlete's social media presence influences their mass media coverage. Some scholars have noted that tenured sports journalists are hesitant to use social media, whereas younger sports reporters are more accepting of these technologies (Schultz & Sheffer, 2010). To that end, perhaps as similarly minded generations of athletes and sports reporters progress in their occupations, social media may be viewed as less threatening, thereby decreasing conflict.

Although social media extends communicative advantages to athletes, athletes must be diligently aware of the wide-reaching effects of their social media messages. With the prestige and glamour that the public places on athletes, it is easy to forget that they are employees or college students. In this regard, messages that the public may view as trivial or for which they may clamor, may violate organizational policies and academic standards. Thus, the organizational implications stemming from social media use by athletes and sports figures is a particularly relevant area for discussion and research.

SOCIAL MEDIA AND SPORTS ORGANIZATIONS

The use of social media is a vitally important issue to which sports organizations must diligently attend. Although public commentary by athletes always has been of some concern to sports organizations, prior to social media, public relations issues were easier to prevent. For instance, the team could allow only friendly journalists to access particular athletes, and employ media and public relations professionals to work with athletes in bolstering their public speaking techniques. As social media can be accessed from virtually any location, sports organizations now have less control over athletes disseminating public messages. Although sports leagues such as the NFL and NBA have adopted social media policies, these measures govern little more than prohibiting athletes from using social media directly before, during, and after games. These policies seem to have limited effectiveness in prompting athletes to use social media strategically. Indeed, there have been multiple occasions where an athlete's social media activity has forced teams to respond quickly to public relations issues, postings that occurred well outside the times prohibited by policy.

One of the more notable cases involved Arizona Cardinals player Darnell Dockett, one of the more consistent Twitter users among professional athletes. On May 14, 2010, Dockett tweeted that he would accept a $1,000 bet to be filmed taking a shower on a webcam. The Cardinals became aware of this scenario and issued a statement to *The Arizona Republic* indicating that the matter was being addressed internally with Dockett (AZcentral.com, 2010). Nevertheless, Dockett filmed the shower and uploaded the video to UStream, a collaborative video filesharing site. It did not take long for this news to circulate across the Internet, and several people responded by posting vivid comments about Dockett's physical anatomy on his Twitter account (comments that since have been removed). Naturally, the Cardinals were not amused by Dockett's actions and on May 18, 2010, Dockett issued a public apology, coupled with acknowledgments by head coach Ken Whisenhunt that Dockett had received counseling about being cautious in his public communications.

Interestingly, Whisenhunt stated that the Cardinals organization wanted its players to use social media as a vehicle to interact with fans, but emphasized that they needed to do so in a manner that reflected positively on the organization. To what extent the Cardinals and other sports organizations define "acceptable" social media use remains unclear. How are such guidelines communicated to athletes? It certainly appears that sports organizations have boundaries that they expect athletes, as employees, not to cross. Although ensuring that these boundaries and guidelines are clear may not entirely prevent troublesome incidents from taking place, it may curb the prevalence with which these issues are currently occurring.

Additionally, by vocalizing organizational expectations for social media use, athletes may be more cautious with their content. On occasion, athletes share emotional messages that appear to have been made in the "heat of the moment." For instance, on September 21, 2009, Robert Henson, a reserve player for the Washington Redskins, tweeted his reaction to fans booing the team during their home game that day. His tweet stated, "you fake half hearted Skins fan can . . . I won't go there but I dislike you very strongly, don't come to Fed Ex to boo dim wits!!" (ESPN.com, 2009b). Interestingly, fans began to criticize Henson via his Twitter account, with some reminding him that he did not play in the game that day and others taking him to task for his comments. Henson then responded with this salvo:

> No I didn't play but I still made more than you in a year and you'd [gladly] switch spots with me in a second. . . . The question is who are you to say you know what's best for the team and you work 9 to 5 at Mcdonalds.

Not surprisingly, the following morning Henson received considerable backlash from the mass media, which required the Redskins to initiate a public response (Henson apologized for his actions and ultimately deactivated his Twitter account). If Henson had insulted fans face to face within the confines of the stadium, the Redskins could have quickly and covertly responded to the aggrieved individuals. However, by conveying these sentiments via Twitter, Henson's audience was significantly magnified, greatly increasing the number of people who could potentially take offense. As this incident suggests, athletes must be cautious in posting critical social media messages, particularly when directed at fans. In such situations, fans and sports reporters obtain a "record" of the offending message, which then is easily publicized. Sports organizations are then caught in reactionary positions as they often are unaware that these messages have been transmitted until they appear in the mass media.

In addition to problematic content, other evidence indicates that athletes are using social media to find groupies with whom they can connect on road trips. This trend provides yet another social media concern for sports organizations. In an article for *ESPN The Magazine*, Kansas City Chiefs player Dwayne Bowe described the practice of "importing":

> You hear stories about groupies hanging out in hotel lobbies, but some of my teammates had it set up so there was a girl in every room. The older guys get on MySpace and Facebook a week before we go to a city; when a pretty one writes back, they arrange to fly her in three or four days in advance. They call it importing.
>
> Anyway, these girls had the whole top floor. They know everything about us—first and last names, sisters and brothers, salary. This one girl was talking to me like she'd known me for years. "Hey, D-Bowe, how's Grandma?" I'm like, "How do you know my grandma?" She knew that I talk about her every time I'm interviewed for a story.
>
> I told her I had a girlfriend, but she didn't care. She was wearing my jersey, sitting in my lap, making it look like we knew each other. Then she took a picture and put it on Facebook. That almost got me in trouble. (Florio, 2010)

Bowe's revelation generated significant media discussion about "importing" and its prevalence in professional sports. Considering the number of athletes who have experienced issues stemming from their interactions with women, this practice is extremely problematic, yet, one that social media makes extremely convenient for athletes to carry out. One only need scroll through many athletes' Twitter followers and Facebook friends to discover that they are composed of vast numbers of women, many of whom have provocative pictures and commentary attached to their user accounts. Additionally, considering the controversy and sanctions that can result when an athlete is alleged to have sexually abused or mistreated a woman, the practice of selecting groupies and arranging to meet up at team hotels is quite risky. This practice may very well be setting up athletes, and thus, sports organizations, for disastrous consequences.

Moreover, those groupies who encounter athletes after connecting on social media can report their liaisons with athletes on their individual social media profiles, creating an additional area of concern for sports organizations. Although athletes certainly accept risks by engaging in this behavior, they may be unaware that photographs and messages have been posted on Facebook, Twitter, or other social media channels, until this content has been publicized. The coordination of athletes and groupies is not a new phenomenon, yet social media offers groupies convenient means to broadcast their experiences with athletes, reports that they can corroborate with pictures. In addition to Facebook and Twitter, the emergence of celebrity gossip Web sites such as TMZ.com and thedirty.com, which seek to distribute "juicy" content about celebrities, further publicize what at the time, may be considered a private activity. As such, it would be prudent for sports organizations to determine the degree to which these practices are occurring with their players and work with players to mitigate the potential for troubling outcomes.

Sports organizations certainly are not the only employers grappling with employees using social media. Indeed, social media is one of the "hot" topics in employment law, and organizations are working to find the balance between protecting the organization and accommodating employees' right to privacy. For instance, when an employer provides an employee with a computer and access to the Internet, does the employee have the right to post content on social media sites during work time? Similarly, if an employer has provided an employee with a cellular phone or laptop, can the employee use these devices to post social media content while not on work time? And perhaps, one of the more pressing questions, to what extent, if at all, should employers be able to access both current and prospective employees' social media profiles?

Employers increasingly are using social media to monitor current employees (e.g., to see if an employee who called in sick has posted status updates on Facebook that reflect otherwise) and as a resource to assess potential employees. Thus, along with the interview, "Googling" an applicant or checking their Facebook and MySpace profiles are becoming standard operating procedure (Elzweig & Peeples, 2009; Sprague, 2007). American labor law is still sorting out precedent to these matters. In the meantime, employers possess the upper hand in using social media to monitor current and prospective employees, and this is certainly the case with sports organizations.

For instance, Orlando Magic player Dwight Howard was fined $35,000 by the NBA for posting critical comments about league officiating on his blog. This disciplinary action is not limited to athletes, but also extends to other nonplaying personnel. For example, Dallas Mavericks owner Mark Cuban has been fined for criticizing league officiating on his blog and Twitter account. Similarly, on April 4, 2009, the Philadelphia Eagles fired Dan Leone, a part-time gate chief at Lincoln Financial Field, after he posted a message on his Facebook profile criticizing the team for not re-signing player Brian Dawkins. Specifically, Leone posted, "Dan is [expletive] devastated about Dawkins signing with Denver . . . Dam Eagles R Retarded!!" (ESPN.com, 2009a). In June 2010, the Pittsburgh Pirates fired Andrew Kurtz, an employee whose job was to dress up in a pierogi costume and run around the stadium. Kurtz's offense? Posting critical commentary on his Facebook page after the Pirates extended the contracts of General Manager Neal Huntington and Manager John Russell (PittsburghChannel.com, 2010). The Pirates soon rehired Kurtz and indicated that such action was because his termination was not in accordance with the team's policy, denying that it was motivated by the public backlash directed at the organization.

Social media clearly have created a number of concerns for sports organizations. Athletes and other team personnel can easily convey information that trigger public relations controversies or which publicly criticizes the organization. Sports organizations seem to have boundaries about acceptable social media use, and how these boundaries are negotiated and communicated to athletes and team personnel may dictate the frequency and intensity of social media content that violates organizational expectations. Indeed, it seems plausible that if sports organizations take an active role in communicating their expectations about social media use to athletes and other employees, mutually beneficial social media practices can be fostered.

One reason that social media have become a paramount issue for sports organizations is that fans are flocking to athletes' social media profiles. Fans now can communicate directly to athletes, and in some cases, engage them in conversation, which has the possibility of turning confrontational (as with Santonio Holmes and Robert Henson). Interestingly, social media has made athletes more accessible virtually, while they correspondingly grow increasingly difficult to access physically. Although fans can interact with athletes through both planned and chance encounters, such opportunities are infrequent, and generally are subject to time and geographic constraints. Social media enables fans and athletes to conveniently interact, providing fans with access that is difficult to obtain otherwise. Thus, social media has produced significant changes in athlete–fan communication, creating new avenues for connection between these two groups.

ATHLETE–FAN COMMUNICATION

Robert Tuchman, president of sports entertainment firm Premiere Corporate Events, observed that "Twitter and other social media programs that connect fans and athletes directly are here to stay. . . . This is an opportunity for athletes to connect directly with their fans and without a third-party intermediary" (J. Miller, 2010). Social media has created significantly more opportunities for fans to directly communicate with athletes. Fans also can access athletes when it is personally convenient, and generally have free reign over message content (although at some point, character and content limits do set in). In fostering this communication, perceptions of closeness with athletes and sports figures increases, leading to several outcomes. For instance, fans can find out where athletes will be and arrange to encounter them, and also engage in parasocial interaction (PSI) with them (Kassing & Sanderson, 2009; Sanderson, 2008c).

Several examples vividly depict these capabilities. On August 26, 2009, cyclist Lance Armstrong, who has an immense Twitter following, tweeted that he would be riding at 5:30 p.m., at a particular intersection in Dublin, Ireland. He closed the tweet by inviting followers to join him. Subsequently, more than 1,000 people showed up (Cromwell, 2009). Armstrong's tweet not only informed fans of his whereabouts, but directly invited them to join him during a training ride. As a result his fans, at least those in Dublin at the time, were presented with an unmatched opportunity to spend time with one of their sporting heroes. Similar occurrences have taken place with other athletes as well. For example, Shaquille O'Neal has tweeted his whereabouts and offered tickets or other prizes to the first person who meets him at that location. In these cases, although limited to certain geographic areas, fans have unique opportunities to meet athletes, a result of invitations that athletes willingly extend through social media.

On April 5, 2010, after his team won the NCAA men's basketball championship, Duke University player Jon Scheyer tweeted his cell phone number. Not surprisingly, he was barraged with a flood of calls, which resulted in him tweeting, "OK my fault . . . Holler at me over Twitter. . . . Stop texting that number pleaseeee." Scheyer was likely caught up in the exhilaration of winning the national championship, but broadcasting his cell phone number provided fans with a way to contact him directly. Although the opportunity to meet athletes can be productive, athletes should be cautious in revealing their whereabouts or contact information. In the wrong hands, such information could promote stalking or other behavior that could endanger the athlete.

In addition to coordinating meetings with fans, athletes also are employing social media to solicit input from fans. For instance, on April 30, 2010, Toronto Raptors player Chris Bosh asked his Twitter followers for their input on his pending free agency. Specifically, Bosh asked, "Where should I go next season and why?" He soon clarified by posting, "Ok. . . . Let me rephrase the question, should I stay or should I go?" To what extent Bosh considered this commentary, if at all, is immaterial, the importance lies in the fact that Twitter enabled fans to respond directly to Bosh's encouragement. Such action promotes feelings of closeness and bonding between fans and athletes. Yet, in other cases, input is not always requested, but nonetheless provided.

Social media allows fans to take a more active role in advising and admonishing athletes. In an earlier work (Sanderson, 2008c), I examined PSI on Boston Red Sox pitcher Curt Schilling's blog and noted that participants frequently advised Schilling on his pitching techniques and also counseled him to ensure that his blogging did not interfere with his athletic performance. Similarly, in Kassing and Sanderson (2009), we observed that fans used cyclist Floyd Landis' blog to offer advice to him ranging from strategies to enhance his cycling competitiveness to activities he should complete postcompetition.

Although much of the interaction occurring between athletes and fans fosters positive communication, some fans use social media to directly voice criticism. The extent to which athletes let such expressions affect them likely varies (Santonio Holmes clearly reached a limit), but social media offers a direct link for fans to convey these feelings to athletes and for athletes to respond to fans. Fans and athletes engaging in verbal conflicts certainly occurs at athletic events, but these incidents are generally limited to fans who are in close proximity to the playing surface. Additionally, security personnel are readily available to separate athletes from fans before the situation escalates (a few notable exceptions of course, including the infamous brawl between Indiana Pacer players and Detroit Piston fans during a game in 2004).

The propensity for fans to contact athletes via social media to rebuke and admonish them may be a manifestation of fan intensity. Research suggests than fans are deeply involved and invested in the performance of athletes and sports teams, often linking their individual worth to the success of these groups (Boyle & Magnusson, 2007; Mean & Kassing, 2008; Wann & Waddill, 2007; Wann & Zaichkowsky, 2009). Accordingly, when athletes engage in behavior that fans deem inappropriate, or which they perceive as affecting team success, social media is a convenient outlet to air these concerns. In more extreme cases, fans can elevate these situations by capturing the private behavior of athletes and reporting these actions across social media channels, leading the sports organization to publicly censure the athlete. For example, in Sanderson (2009a), I examined how fans used social media to alert sports organizations to the conduct of three professional athletes (NBA players Josh Howard and Greg Oden, and NFL player Matt

Leinart). Interestingly, all three incidents took place on these athletes' personal time, with one incident taking place at the athlete's home (Leinart). Yet, the reports were framed in ways that emphasized the player's behavior as being detrimental to team success. Thus, these fans saw it as their duty to broadcast these actions. These types of incidents are more likely to occur in the future, as the private behaviors of athletes and sports figures become increasingly public.

With these examples and discussion providing the underlying structure, I now proceed to a more thorough treatment of social media and its affect on sports media, sports organizations, and fan–athlete interactions. The vast impact that social media has introduced into the sport world is impressive. As communication technologies continue to evolve, these implications will only become more numerous. As a result, diligent vigilance in monitoring and responding to these trends will be crucial.

2

SOCIAL MEDIA AS SPORTS MEDIA

The Internet has greatly transformed sports media, ushering in an era where sports news and information is available on demand. It was not that long ago that limited options were available for sports news—purchasing the newspaper, subscribing to sports magazines such as *Sports Illustrated* or *The Sporting News*, or viewing sports segments on the evening newscast. In 1979, ESPN was launched, significantly increasing the availability of sports media—albeit for those who purchased cable television. Throughout the 1980s and 1990s, sports talk radio grew more prevalent, ESPN expanded its programming networks (e.g., ESPN2, ESPN radio, ESPN The Magazine), and ESPN competitors such as Fox Sports also started their own television and radio networks.

Although these developments greatly enhanced the availability of sports media, they seem to pale in comparison to the changes introduced by the Internet. Indeed, diverse sports content is more accessible than ever before and production is no longer limited to established mass media organizations, a capability that is in part, attributable to social media. For example, athletes can exert more control over their public portrayals and directly counter mass media reports. Prior to exploring these outcomes in more detail, a summary of the Internet's effect on sports media is offered here.

The leveling of the sports media hierarchy is one of the most evident changes that the Internet has generated in sports media. The Internet creates opportunities for those outside the mainstream media to produce sports media content. This capability then provides audiences with diverse avenues to select from when consuming sports media. Sports media scholars Brett Hutchins and David Rowe (2009) referred to this transformation as constituting a shift from "broadcast scarcity" to an era of "digital plenitude" (p. 354). They further contend that the broadcasting capabilities offered by the Internet, "demands adjustment and reorganization in both media and sports industries" (p. 355) and observe that the Internet extinguishes the notion that there is a "scarcity" of sports media channels. As a result, media organizations are experiencing tremendous changes, a trend that is visibly apparent in the newspaper industry. Some newspapers have been unable to compete with their "digital-only" competitors, prompting many newspapers to fold, convert to an "online-only" approach, or merge the two into a hybrid business model.

The list of newspapers that have ceased operations or incorporated these approaches contains some very recognizable names: *The Seattle Post-Intelligencer, Rocky Mountain News, Christian Science Monitor, Detroit News/Detroit Free Press,* and *The East Valley (AZ) Tribune* (Lieberman, 2009). Additionally, some media outlets have phased out sports reporting entirely. For instance, on December 31, 2009, *The Washington Times* announced that it was ceasing operation of its sports department (Elfin, 2009). The *Times* maintained a Web-based sports page and is a well-established periodical, so this decision was somewhat surprising. This phenomena, however, suggests that traditional sports media sources are growing less relevant and competitive with sports media consumers. Digital sports media sites can be operated very cost efficiently, and are well positioned to cater to sports media consumers who are increasingly turning to the Internet for sports information. Thus, the ability to instantaneously provide sports news coupled with a relatively inexpensive operating structure may be placing traditional, "print-only" sports media organizations at an extreme competitive disadvantage.

Although some media sectors have been impacted by the Internet's emergence, elite mass media organizations still maintain prominence—ESPN is not going away anytime soon. Yet, the Internet increases competition even for these organizations as other entities can now break sports news, which pulls audience members to their sites. For example, consider the NFL Draft, a widely covered media event (Mercurio & Filak, 2010; Oates, 2009). One of the most popular activities leading up to the Draft occurs when media pundits predict which college athletes NFL teams will select and offer commentary on athletes whose "stock" is moving "up" or "down." This ritual has predominantly been relegated to "experts" such as

ESPN's Mel Kiper Jr.; however, one only need Google the term "NFL Mock Draft" to find a multitude of sites offering NFL Draft predictions and analysis authored by individuals who are outside the mainstream media. Although ESPN and other elite mass media organizations still maintain primacy in NFL Draft coverage, the readership on some of these sites allows the owners to generate revenue by selling advertising to major corporations. These individuals are now competing with established sports journalists and media personalities to determine who is more accurate in predicting the NFL Draft.

Although many independent sports media sites may be inconsequential to established sports media organizations, several sites have put these elite mass media organizations on notice. These entities benefit from an unconventional reporting structure that enables them to distribute stories without the same verifications processes that govern most mass media organizations. For example, consider Profootballtalk.com. The "About" section of their Web site contains the following declaration:

> We don't have editors, we don't have agendas, we don't owe anyone anything, and we don't care. As a result, we're beholden to no one. We do this because we love pro football, and we love bringing you the truth.

Several paragraphs later is this interesting contention:

> We're the first to admit that we don't always adhere to pure journalistic standards. We don't seek reactions from players, coaches, and/or agents before posting controversial stories. However, we'll give anyone who objects to one of our stories an opportunity to respond. And we won't run anything that we know or have reason to know is untrue.

Despite their pronouncement that journalistic standards are not always followed, Profootballtalk.com has slowly gained mainstream acceptance from both the NFL and mainstream mass media outlets. In fact, the editor of Profootballtalk.com, Mike Florio, who is an attorney by trade, is a frequent guest on prominent sports radio talk shows. On June 15, 2009, Profootballtalk.com announced it was becoming an affiliate of NBC Sports, a credential that further enhanced the site's legitimacy. On a surface level, this announcement may seem immaterial, yet it demonstrates how amateur sports media sites compete with and rival mainstream media outlets. In this particular case, Profootballtalk.com's popularity prompted a prominent news organization to partner with an amateur site, a move that only a decade ago would have seemed preposterous.

Although Profootballtalk.com has forged symbiotic relationships with established sports media organizations, another popular sports blog—Deadspin.com, has taken a different approach. Deadspin is one of the most highly viewed sports news blogs and reports information about athletes' game performances and increasingly, their private lives (Clavio, 2009). Deadspin has a contentious relationship with established mass media organizations, and has taken particular delight in criticizing ESPN. For instance, in 2008, founding editor Will Leitch penned a book entitled *God Save the Fan: How Steroid Hypocrites, Soul Sucking Suits, and a Worldwide Leader Not Named Bush Have Taken the Fun Out of Sports*. One of the sections of this book is devoted to critiquing ESPN's self-promotion, including a chapter entitled "Ten Examples of How ESPN Is Ruining Sports" (Clavio, 2009).

Although Leitch has since left Deadspin, the conflict between the two organizations continues. One visible incident occurred in October 2009, when A.J. Daulerio, Deadspin's current editor, perceived that ESPN had misled him about its decision to terminate baseball analyst Steve Phillips for sexual misconduct with a programming staffer (Gregory, 2009). Apparently, Daulerio had been aware of Phillips' sexual relations with this employee approximately 1 month before the story was finally reported in the *New York Post*. Daulerio was upset that ESPN had not dealt in a forthright manner with him about this issue. In response, he launched a blog post entitled "ESPN Horndog Dossier" in which he claimed he would reveal all the rumors Deadspin had received about sexual interactions between ESPN personalities and staffers (Gregory, 2009). Not surprisingly, ESPN was outraged and this incident prompted questions about journalistic integrity and standards. Indeed, organizations such as ESPN have more pressure to report accurate information and are more invested in relationships with professional sports leagues and athletes. These conditions are less stringent for independent sites, which may fuel their propensity to publish questionable stories.

The preceding examples introduce several important implications for sports media. For instance, consider Profootballtalk.com's proclamation that the site is not beholden to any person or entity in its sports reporting (although the site's affiliation with NBC suggests that this statement may not hold the veracity it once did). What are the consequences of such a philosophy? Clearly, most independent sites are likely committed to verifying their stories, but it also seems plausible that they might "run" with reports prior to solidifying verification to become the initial outlet to report the story. Mainstream mass media organizations generally must have at least one and often two confirmations from sources for a story to be publicly reported. If independent sports media sites are reporting these stories with minimal source verification, they may gain the upper hand with sports media consumers.

The need to corroborate reports is certainly understandable, and not all stories possess the same degree of importance. However, if these independent sites are consistently breaking major sports news, regardless of accuracy, it may increase their credibility with audience members. Indeed, research suggests that some people perceive blogs to be as credible as mainstream media sources (Flanagin & Metzger, 2000; Johnson & Kaye, 2004; Johnson, Kaye, Bichard, & Wong, 2007) and thus, people may be more influenced by content than accuracy. Clearly, disseminating multiple reports in the hopes that something "sticks" is a troublesome journalistic approach. Yet, given the growing popularity of these independent sites, legitimacy does not appear to be an overwhelming concern for sports media consumers.

As independent sites grow more popular, the popularity of stories about athletes' private behavior has dramatically increased, producing an important shift in sports media reporting. Although sites such as Deadspin report news of this nature, there are other domains specifically dedicated to broadcasting athletes' public indiscretions such as drunkathlete.com, and thedirty.com. As if these sites needed competition, celebrity gossip site TMZ.com has announced plans to launch a Web site devoted solely to gossip about athletes and their private behavior—TMZsports.com (Sandomir, 2009). Gossip about athletes and sport figures currently occupies a prominent portion of the TMZ Web site, and there is no shortage of information about athletes' private behavior available online.

The growth of these sites suggests that a public demand exists for this content, and scholars have noted that sports journalism is increasingly mimicking celerity journalism (Rowe, 2007; Whannel, 2001). Although athletes and sports figures should not be excused for illegal behavior, at some point, the growing coverage of their private lives becomes problematic. Furthermore, considering that people can document athletes' and sports figures' behavior with miniscule mobile devices and cameras, these individuals may be unaware that their private actions are being captured for public consumption. Additionally, sites such as TMZ encourage audience members to report on athletes and sports figures, reinforcing their celebrity journalism traits (Fink, Parker, Brett, & Higgins, 2009).

Although mainstream media organizations must now attend to competition from independent media sites, through social media, athletes and other sports figures also are emerging as a competitive force. Athletes are turning to social media, particularly blogs and Twitter to break news, provide commentary on other news stories (both inside and outside of sports), and to contest perceived inaccurate portrayals by sports reporters. Before turning to exemplars of this trend, a rationale for why these social media capabilities have become prominent is warranted.

Athletes and sports journalists have long had a symbiotic relationship. Athletes were dependent on sports reporters to generate stories about them, thereby increasing their public visibility. As this publicity grew, athletes obtained and maintained celebrity status and its accompanying benefits (e.g., endorsement deals). Similarly, sports journalists needed athletes to provide quotes and storylines so they could author compelling articles to give them a competitive advantage over other news outlets. Each party entered this relationship accepting tradeoffs. Athletes needed press attention to maintain public viability, yet this benefit was tempered by sports reporters framing articles about athletes in certain ways to guide public interpretation (Sanderson, 2008; Weaver, McCombs, & Shaw, 2004). Framing occurs as reporters interject their personal opinions into the story, shaping audience perceptions that are sometimes unfavorable to the athlete. On the other hand, journalists, particularly "beat writers" (reporters who are designated by a media organization to cover a local team), spend significant time with players as they travel with the team. As a result, they often are exposed to private indiscretions that generally are withheld from the public to preserve the athlete's trust.

Whereas athletes needed reporters for promotion, the acceptance of negative framing often led to animosity toward journalists. As athletes still needed public platforms, there was little recourse for them to address their grievances—until social media burst on the scene. With social media tools, athletes no longer need journalists to maintain a high public presence. Indeed, social media can be employed to directly connect with fans and to contest perceived negative framing and inaccuracies in media reporting. Moreover, with the integrative capabilities offered by social media, athletes can involve fans in their efforts to combat sports reporters. As such, these communication tools become valuable public relations tools that athletes can use to foster support for their views and positions. Considering the ways that framing occurs in sports media, these are tremendous advantages for athletes.

For instance, R. Bishop (2005) chronicled local press coverage of Seattle Seahawks wide receiver Joey Galloway during his 1999 training camp holdout as he attempted to renegotiate his contract. Bishop observed that sports reporters framed Galloway as an immature individual who was abdicating his responsibility to the team. He also found that journalists framed the team as a sacred entity whose collective value superseded the worth of any one individual. Furthermore, while framing Galloway in these ways, sports journalists alternatively framed the head coach as a revered organizational figure whose authority is unquestionable. Thus, audience members were stimulated to think about Galloway as a selfish, immature, individual, rather than thinking about why his holdout may have been warranted. Commentary of this nature is consistently applied to athletes who hold out in efforts to renegotiate their contracts (R. Bishop, 2005).

In such situations, sports reporters quickly label these athletes as "complainers" and "whiners," and as being "selfish." Consider this commentary by journalist Kent Somers (2010), The *Arizona Republic*'s beat writer who covers the Arizona Cardinals. In discussing offensive lineman Deuce Lutui's absence from a 3-day minicamp, amidst disagreements about a long-term contract, Somers opined:

> The best offensive linemen understand the importance of leverage, how to gain it and use it to their advantage. While Cardinals guard Deuce Lutui has improved at implementing the concept on the field in recent years, it's eluding him off of it.

Lutui ultimately signed a 1-year contract with the Cardinals. This article, however, positions Lutui as lacking requisite intelligence to manage his contractual situation and frames the football field as the only place where he can use his mental faculties to gain leverage. As these attributions were consumed by audience members, they prompted perceptions that Lutui was selfish and not committed to the team. Contract and compensation issues are easy fodder for sports journalists. Although athletes are certainly well paid, many of them have short playing careers (indeed in the NFL, once a player reaches 30, he is considered to be on the downside of his career) and must maximize their earning power. The public is not privy to athletes' rationales for engaging in holdouts and contract disputes, but the reliability of sports reporters framing these actions in negative ways is certain. Whereas in the past athletes were reliant on sports reporters to counter these framings, social media endows them with the broadcast capabilities to challenge these representations. Moreover, as they offer reasoning for their actions, this communication may facilitate public acceptance and support for their decisions (Sanderson, 2010).

As athletes more consistently use social media to break news and communicate with fans, sports journalists may become less relevant as conduits to connect fans and athletes. Not surprisingly, sports journalists are increasingly attacking their newfound competition. This often plays out by reporters framing athletes' social media use as a team distraction that reflects a selfish character. Former Boston Red Sox pitcher Curt Schilling, a very active social media user, was a frequent target of sports journalists for his blogging. Schilling was well known for his candor, and did not hide his feelings and convictions when communicating both face to face and via his blog—38pitches.com. A few examples depict the stigma that some press members attached to Schilling's social media activity.

For instance, Schilling was labeled a "Beantown Blabbermouth" (Madden, 2007); as "Stubborn Schilling stealing the spotlight" (Brewer, 2007b); and a "self-righteous pitcher" (Brewer, 2007a). Such framings perpetuate notions that athletes who use social media are selfish, greedy, and not committed to their team. Sports journalists then capitalize on these interpretations to protect their relevance with sports media consumers. Nevertheless, athletes' social media sites grow more popular. In Schilling's case, blog readers were quite supportive of his social media use and encouraged him to continue blogging (Sanderson, 2010). Thus, although sports reporters unfavorably describe athletes' social media activity, these critiques may actually foster fan support, which then increases athletes' use of these communicative channels.

The capability for social media to counter press inaccuracies will not eliminate negative framing. However, it does offer a viable mechanism for athletes to "fight back" and dispute mass media reporting, which may hold sports reporters more accountable for their commentary. Furthermore, in contesting these reports, athletes also take advantage of another important social media benefit—optimizing self-presentation (Bargh, McKenna, & Fitzsimons, 2002; Dominick, 1999; Kim & Papacharissi, 2003). In more actively managing their public image via social media, athletes can disclose news at their convenience and maintain significant control over the structures of these messages. Accordingly, the chapter now discusses some ways that both athletes and sports figures are using social media to accomplish these purposes.

BREAKING NEWS AND PROVIDING COMMENTARY

Whereas the mass media still holds primacy in reporting stories, social media enables athletes and sports figures to circumvent the media and directly break news via their social media account. One of the foremost ways that this trend is manifesting is with athletes who are free agents using social media to broadcast the franchise with whom they will sign. For instance, on September 9, 2009, NBA superstar Allen Iverson, a free agent at the time, informed fans via his Twitter feed, that he was signing a contract with the Memphis Grizzlies franchise (*Toronto Sun*, 2009). On March 6, 2010, Seattle Seahawks free agent wide receiver Nate Burleson announced on Twitter that he had signed with the Detroit Lions—"It's official so 'Go Lions.'" On April 5, 2010, Philadelphia Eagles quarterback Donovan McNabb, who had been the subject of rampant trade rumors tweeted his new destination after finally being traded, "Helloooo Washington."

On November 1, 2010, Phoenix Suns forward Jared Dudley tweeted, "Yes Suns fans!!!!" 5 yr. Max deal!!!!!!! Lol ok not max but a fair and good deal..Glad to be apart of this org future." The next day Dudley posted this tweet, "Working Hard to reach a lifetime goal of signing a 5 yr deal with

The PHX SUNS!! Priceless!" Within this tweet, Dudley embedded a link to a photograph of him signing his contract. The ability for athletes and sports figures to supplement their social media profiles with pictures offers fans additional insights into their lives that promote intimacy and closeness. Other notable examples include Miami Heat player LeBron James posting his son's kindergarten cubby on his Twitter feed and Cincinnati Bengals player Terrell Owens posting his dormitory room at the Bengals training camp. These disclosures give fans "insider" access that is difficult to obtain from other venues (Kassing & Sanderson, 2010).

Social media certainly offers athletes in transition between franchises unique capabilities to keep fans informed of their progress and ultimate playing destinations. Beyond these messages, however, social media also may become more prominent for athletes to broadcast career decisions. This potential was dramatically illustrated by Schilling on March 23, 2009, when he announced that he was retiring from Major League Baseball (MLB)—via his blog. Schilling entitled the posting "Calling it quits," discussed some of his career achievements, and expressed gratitude to those who had helped him succeed in his professional career:

> To say I've been blessed would be like calling Refrigerator Perry "a bit overweight." The things I was allowed to experience, the people I was able to call friends, teammates, mentors, coaches and opponents, the travel, all of it, are far more than anything I ever thought possible in my lifetime.
>
> Four World Series, three World Championships. That there are men with plaques in Cooperstown who never experienced one—and I was able to be on three teams over seven years that won it all—is another "beyond my wildest dreams" set of memories I'll take with me.
>
> The game always gave me far more than I ever gave it. All of those things, every single one of those memories is enveloped with fan sights and sounds for me. Without the fans, they would still be great memories, but none would be enduring and unforgettable because they infused the energy, rage, passion and "feel" of all of those times. The game was here long before I was, and will be here long after I'm gone. The only thing I hope I did was never put in question my love for the game, or my passion to be counted on when it mattered most. I did everything I could to win every time I was handed the ball.
>
> I am and always will be more grateful than any of you could ever possibly know.
>
> I want to offer two special thank you's.
>
> To my Lord and Savior Jesus Christ for granting me the ability to step between the lines for 23 years and compete against the best players in the world.

To my wife Shonda and my 4 children, Gehrig, Gabriella, Grant and Garrison for sacrificing their lives and allowing baseball to be mine while I played. Without their unquestioned support I would not have been able to do what I did, or enjoy the life, and I am hopefully going to live long enough to repay them as much as a Father and Husband can.

Thank you and God Bless

Curt Schilling

Historically an athlete's retirement announcement is accompanied by significant pomp and circumstance. Sports organizations often construct elaborate press conferences where the athlete issues a retirement statement and then responds to questions from sports reporters. Considering that Schilling was an active social media participant during his playing career and had contentious relationships with some sports reporters, it is not surprising that he elected to disclose his retirement on his blog. By announcing his retirement through social media, he was able to avoid conflict with sports reporters about his playing career, legacy, and chances for the Baseball Hall of Fame.

Additionally, Schilling was able to present his message directly to fans without filtering from sports journalists or the sports organization. If Schilling solely relied on a press conference to convey this message, as reports of this event emerged, journalists' framings may have influenced public interpretations of Schilling's career. Such framings may have prompted fans to remember Schilling in ways that perhaps, were unfavorable toward him. Thus, blogging his retirement enabled Schilling to maintain complete control over this important message, allowing fans to both consume the message *and* communicate directly to him about his announcement (there were 1,261 replies). This unprecedented participative opportunity would have been unavailable to fans had this message been disclosed via a traditional press conference.

The extent to which significant announcements such as career retirements transcend to social media remains to be seen. To some degree this may depend on, among others, the caliber of the athlete (e.g., superstar, role player), the relational history between the athlete, the sports organization, and sports reporters, and the athlete's social media presence (high or low user). It is possible that Schilling's announcement will be an anomaly; yet, the potential also exists for other athletes to employ social media for such events. Moreover, while Schilling's retirement announcement and fan responses were communicated asynchronously, in the future, athletes may broadcast such announcements in "real time" and invite questions from fans using social media. Through social media, whether asynchronously or synchronously, athletes can integrate fans into their communicative messages, thereby shifting media interactions into the hands of fans and away from journalists and reporters.

Social media also have become very popular for amateur athletes, and they too are using these tools to disseminate news. For example, on April 24, 2010, Stafon Johnson, a former University of Southern California (USC) football player, used Twitter to announce that he had signed with the Tennessee Titans after not being selected in the 2010 NFL Draft. Johnson tweeted, "Thankyu jesus the lord is good yu kan find me in cashvillee aka nashville imma titan." Johnson's social media use is particularly noteworthy considering his personal circumstances. During the 2009 football season, Johnson was nearly killed while completing bench press weight training. While Johnson was lifting, the bar slipped, crushing his neck and larynx. Johnson needed emergency surgery, and while his life was saved, he has experienced difficulty regaining his speaking abilities. Thus, for Johnson, social media was very beneficial as he could publicly communicate without having to physically speak (Interestingly, after this incident, then USC head coach Pete Carroll used Twitter to encourage fans to keep Johnson in their prayers; ESPN.com, 2009c).

Nonplaying sports personalities are jumping into the social media world and connecting with fans as well. Seattle Seahawks head coach Pete Carroll regularly keeps fans abreast of team news via his Twitter postings. Carroll is quite ingenious with his postings, and one of the more unique ways he employed Twitter occurred during the 2010 NFL Draft. Carroll tweeted popular culture references as hints to reveal the player the Seahawks would be selecting. Fans responded to Carroll via Twitter with their answer to the clue. This "game" became quite popular and several sports media personalities even joined in this activity. Additionally, prominent NFL agent Drew Rosenhaus uses Twitter to broadcast news about his clients. This became particularly relevant in the days leading up to the NFL Draft, as Rosenhaus employed Twitter to generate interest in his clients. For example, on March 1, 2010, "Congrats to RSR client Jason Pierre Paul who ran a 4.6 forty at 270lbs and solidified his spot in the top 10 of the 1st round!" Then on March 3, 2010, "University of Arizona tight end Rob Gronkowski will hold a full work out for NFL teams on March 27th in Tucson." Thus, for sports figures such as coaches, general managers, and agents, social media enables them to give fans "insider" perspectives about team and player news (Kassing & Sanderson, 2010). For player agents, social media is an optimal venue to promote their clients. Agents can broadcast intricate details to a number of vested parties about diverse topics such as athletic performance, training regiment, and community service. In doing so, they visibly highlight the player's "selling points."

Although playing-related news is a prominent social media topic, athletes also are disclosing personal news via these channels. For instance, Lance Armstrong used Twitter to announce the impending birth of his fifth child. Interestingly, Armstrong disclosed this information by creating and following a Twitter profile for the unborn child with the username "@Cincoarmstrong." Armstrong then posted a status update from this account declaring, "I got 2 arms, 2 legs, a nickname, and 2 inches long. See y'all in October." Fans began bombarding Armstrong's Twitter profile with questions about this new follower and Armstrong finally confirmed their suspicions. His tweet declared, "Getting ?'s today about someone I'm following, a certain @Cincoarmstrong. What to say? Yet another blessing in our lives. I cannot wait!" (People.com, 2010).

Additionally, former MLB players Jose Canseco and Roger Clemens have used Twitter to broadcast aspects of their involvement with federal investigations into performance-enhancing drug use in MLB. On March 23, 2010, Canseco announced on Twitter that he had been subpoenaed to appear before a grand jury investigating Clemens' alleged performance-enhancing drug use (Associated Press, 2010c). Clemens used Twitter to fight allegations that he used performance-enhancing drugs during his playing career. For example, on August 19, 2010, "I never took HGH or Steroids. And I did not lie to Congress. I look forward to challenging the Governments." Then on August 26, 2010, "Thanks so much for the calls, emails, and texts and tweets. Many many thx." Whereas Canseco used Twitter for informative purposes, Twitter provided Clemens with a public forum where he could battle detractors and express gratitude to his supporters. Furthermore, through Twitter he tailored messages that represented his views and promoted fans to continue their support, even expressing gratitude directly to several followers for their encouragement.

Social media also is becoming a popular way for athletes and sports figures to broadcast commentary, particularly with respect to player movement. Traditionally, when players changed teams, sports reporters generally sought commentary from select players. Although this still occurs, any player with a social media account can weigh in on such matters. For example, on April 2, 2010, Arizona Cardinals player Kerry Rhodes tweeted, "welcome my homey @jayfeely to the squad just like u did me he's a super dude!!" Similarly, when the New York Jets acquired wide receiver Santonio Holmes from the Pittsburgh Steelers, Jets cornerback Derrelle Revis tweeted, "Wow we got holmes this is crazy. We makin big moves this off-season. Putting the pieces together to get closer to that superbowl ring."

Social media further enables athletes to offer commentary about aspects of competition that are unlikely to reach public view through mainstream media reporting. In Kassing and Sanderson (2010), we explored how cyclists participating in the 2009 Tour of Italy used Twitter to communicate their feelings about various competition components. Examples included:

Crazy finish today! Peloton [term used to refer to the group of riders] was going over 70 mph through twisty, small roads. Its safe to say the giro keeps you on our toes (Tom Danielson, May 14).

Wow, the last 30km was crazy! The peloton was not happy (Levi Leipheimer, May 14).

Done with stage 6. Uh ... wow. That was the craziest last 30k I've ever seen. Long, fast decent at 80k (50mph) plus then a tight circuit (Lance Armstrong, May 14).

Not sure that's necessary really. Tomorrow is the same kind of finish. It's bike racing, not moto gp. (Lance Armstrong, May 14).

Didn't enjoy the last decent into the finish. Dangerous stuff :-/ (Michael Rogers, May 15).

In truth it only rained the final 90mins. But the 25 mile gnarly descent in the pissing rain, I could have happily done without (Ted King, May 15).

Holy sh*tballs that was a ridiculous finish. Someone was not thinking when they came up with that (Tom Danielson, May 15).

Done with st 7 [stage 7]. I've seen it all now. 25 mile fast decent to the finish. In the pissing rain. Makes no sense. The boys in the bunch are ... Livid (Lance Armstrong, May 15). (pp. 120-121)

Using social media to offer commentary on player movements may seem mundane, yet it allows athletes to divulge their opinions on topic in which they have vested interests. Although much of this commentary is positive, if a player was genuinely upset about a teammate leaving, publicly airing these feelings could create problems for the sports organization. Additionally, players from competing teams have had Twitter "arguments," and if these individuals found themselves on the same team, these past actions could escalate conflict. Whereas sharing input on player movements may only occasionally become controversial, athletes are turning to social media to broadcast their opinions on various news stories outside the sports realm. This behavior has significant potential to ignite controversy and generate press attention is much greater.

One notable example that prompted a number of athletes to comment on a political issue occurred on April 24, 2010. On that date, Arizona Gov. Jan Brewer signed into state law Senate Bill 1070, a bill that was labeled as the "nation's toughest bill on illegal immigration" (Archibold, 2010). As Brewer signed this bill, a floodgate of controversy followed, and athletes were not shy about weighing in on the debate. One of the more overt responses from the sports world occurred on May 3, 2010, when the Phoenix Suns elected to alter their uniforms for their playoff game that night against the San Antonio Spurs. The Suns changed their jersey to say "Los Suns" as a show of support for the Arizona Hispanic community.

Phoenix Suns player Amare Stoudemire subsequently tweeted about this decision, "We support the Latin community. They are apart of the 12 tribes of Israel. It's 1 Nation under YAH (god). Shalom. Los Suns." Similarly, Baltimore Ravens wide receiver Donte Stallworth, tweeted, "I'm so happy the Los Suns of Phoenix are doing this tonight ... Way to go Mr. Robert Sarva!! [Suns owner]" Stallworth had previously commented about the law on April 30, 2010, "Nazi Germany: "show me your papers!!" I'm sure it'll be equipped w/RFID chip also ... the ole banana in the tail pipe." This law is still causing considerable controversy, and the sports world has found itself heavily involved in the debate over this issue. In addition to public responses from athletes broadcast via both traditional and social media, ESPN.com offered Brewer a forum to express her rationale for the law. Given ESPN's large market size, this was a valuable opportunity for Brewer to convey her views. Indeed, calls have been made for MLB to remove the 2011 All-Star game from Phoenix, and other sports leagues have been called on to boycott Arizona. Although this debate certainly played out both in physical demonstrations and via mass media outlets, social media became an important vehicle for athletes to express their views on the issue.

Athletes can certainly voice opinions about political issues through traditional press outlets. Yet, given the tension that surrounds these topics, teams may encourage athletes to refrain from commenting or temper their reactions. In using social media, athletes can more readily express their views outside the team's control, which may prompt them to become more involved in social issues. Moreover, expressing their views and exerting their influence to persuade the public to align with their views may become a resource for both advocacy and political groups to consider.

It seems plausible that social media will grow more viable as a tool for athletes to offer commentary about political and social issues. As this trend grows, a number of questions will need to be explored. For instance, do athletes become more overt in their political and social commentary? If so, what are the ramifications for both athletes and sports organizations? Social media clearly have opened avenues for athletes to become more active in breaking and distributing news stories, a capability that both reduces their reliance on sports journalists and increases their connections with fans. Although the significance of this news varies, it nonetheless brings more balance to the sports media hierarchy. As athletes become more involved in news production, they also become more active in managing their public presentation. Indeed, social media is a prime venue to contest perceived biases and inaccuracies in sports media reporting.

COUNTERING NEGATIVE FRAMING AND MEDIA INACCURACIES

Sports journalists often frame athletes in ways that are unfavorable to the athlete. Historically, athletes have had some recourse to contest these actions, such as directly confronting reporters or seeking out more sympathetic press members. However, these actions generally exacerbate tensions between athletes and reporters and fuel public perceptions that the athlete is a "whiner." Framing has been greatly magnified with the emergence of speculative journalism, as athletes and sports figures must constantly address rumors and private matters that are reported in media outlets. Continually addressing these questions may be "part of the job," but surely becomes tiring, and social media allows athletes and sports figures with a convenient and less threatening mechanism to address these reports.

For instance, Clemens used his Twitter account to respond to a *New York Daily News* article that reported comments by his ex-mistress, country singer Mindy McCready. McCready had suggested Clemens had experienced decreased sexual effectiveness as a result of using performance-enhancing drugs. In response, Clemens tweeted, "and BTW ... I've taking great care of my body and to this date and time all the pipes on this body are still working great. Thx for asking" (Vinton, 2010). Clemens has been the subject of multiple allegations that he used performance-enhancing drugs during his playing career, and on a previous occasion he attempted to address these allegations via a traditional press conference. However, after becoming visibly frustrated by reporters' questions, Clemens abruptly ended the conference. For Clemens, social media allowed him to comment on this report without having to invest energies in scheduling a press conference. Given the outcome of his last press conference, such an event likely would have produced substantial conflict with sports reporters.

Similarly, former Arizona Cardinals quarterback Kurt Warner used Twitter to respond to rumors that he was considering resuming his playing career, "Why does everyone think I am coming back? Do I have the wrong definition of 'retirement' or has it been changed in recent years?" Warner could have called a press conference or contacted sports radio stations to address these reports, however, social media allowed him to quickly and conveniently respond to these rumors without causing significant life disruptions. In this respect, social media has become an invaluable resource for athletes and other sports figures to respond to rumors. As competition for sports media consumers grows more intense and speculative journalism increases, social media is a tremendous way to diffuse such reports. Sports journalists certainly will continue to ask athletes and sports figures to address speculation, but social media is now a source to which they can refer these questions.

Moreover, by employing social media to rebuff perceived negative framing and journalistic inaccuracies, athletes gain access to empathetic audiences who often support their positions. One of the more poignant examples where this occurred happened with Schilling. During the 2004 American League Championship Series (ALCS) the Red Sox were battling back from a seemingly insurmountable three-game deficit against their archrival, the New York Yankees. Having won two consecutive games, the Red Sox entered Game 6 at Yankee Stadium in a must-win situation. Schilling had been plagued by ankle injuries and was scheduled to start Game 6. Prior to the game, he underwent an experimental surgery in which his ankle tendons were sutured together (Mariotti, 2004).

While Schilling was pitching during the game, his ankle began bleeding through his sock. Schilling nevertheless remained in the game and delivered a masterful performance that greatly contributed to the Red Sox winning 4 to 2. Schilling's performance was praised by sports journalists as "legendary" and his efforts earned the admiration of the Red Sox fan base, affectionately known as "Red Sox Nation" (Mariotti, 2004). The Red Sox subsequently won the ALCS and Schilling's ankle again bled during a brilliant pitching performance in the World Series against the St. Louis Cardinals. This performance seemed to propel the Red Sox to a World Series title as they beat the Cardinals in four straight games.

The bloody sock soon became established as a symbol by Red Sox players and fans. Indeed the sock signified the team's resilience and determination in coming back to beat the Yankees and ending an 86-year World Series drought (Connolly, 2007). Almost 3 years later, on April 25, 2007, during a game between the Red Sox and the Baltimore Orioles, the authenticity of the bloody sock was questioned. Orioles play-by-play commentator Gary Thorne alleged that Red Sox catcher Doug Mirabelli had informed him that Schilling's bloody sock was faked and that Schilling had painted his sock as a publicity stunt. These comments rapidly permeated across media outlets and Thorne immediately retracted his comments, stating that he had misunderstood Mirabelli. Mirabelli, however, was quite irate, and declared that his comments to Thorne were in jest, and that Thorne was fully aware of this intent. Schilling also was understandably upset, as his athletic and moral integrity had been publicly questioned. Yet, rather than engaging Thorne directly about the incident other than stating "It gets stupider" (Edes, 2007, p. C1), Schilling responded by blogging. On April 27, 2007 Schilling posted a blog entry entitled "Ignorance has its privileges" a 1,549-word open letter to fans, in which he lambasted Thorne and directed criticism toward specific sports journalists and media coverage in general.

In Sanderson (2008a), I examined how Schilling used this entry to "turn the tables" and criticize sports journalists with statements such as:

> Instead of using the forums they participate in to do something truly different, change lives, inspire people, you have an entire subset of media whose sole purpose in life is to actually be the news, instead of report it. (p. 921)

> If you haven't figured it out by now, working in the media is a pretty nice gig. Barring outright plagiarism or committing a crime, you don't have to be accountable if you don't want to. You can say what you want when you want and you don't really have to answer to anyone. You can always tell the bigger culprits by the fact you never see their faces in the clubhouse. Most of them are afraid to show themselves to the subjects they rail on everyday. (p. 922)

Schilling then noted one of the primary functions of his blog:

> So for one of the first times this blog serves one of the purposes I'd hoped it would if the need arose. The media hacked and spewed their way to a day or two of stories that had zero basis in truth. A story fabricated by the media, for the media. The best part was that instead of having to sit through a litany of interviews to "defend" myself, or my teammates, I got to do that here. (p. 923)

This particular observation highlights one of the most compelling reasons for athletes to use social media—combating media inaccuracies. With social media, athletes can immediately contest press reports without having to rely on reporters to disseminate these messages to the public. Relying on journalists as a conduit to publicize frustration with media inaccuracies is unlikely to provide desired remediation and may lead to further framing, exaggeration and misinterpretation. Social media allows athletes to respond to sports journalists at their convenience and to maintain control over message presentation.

In Schilling's case, directly criticizing sports journalists was a significant shift in sports media production. Although athletes do complain about journalists during interviews, social media allows them to assertively construct and broadcast their views, essentially becoming sports media critics. This commentary also benefits from fan participation that enables athletes to foster audience support. In response to Schilling's media criticisms, audience members were very empathetic. Examples included: "i still agree with you when it comes to the media fabricating stories and not focusing on anything important," "You are right on about the media. They have no talent and no one would know who they were if they didn't make up stupid stories like this," "As for ESPN, they're the biggest frauds" and "I hate the media with a passion. They are extremely ignorant and have as much use on a deserted island as a lawyer—shark food!" (Sanderson, 2008a, p. 923). In contesting perceived media inaccuracies within highly encouraging forums, social media sites are valuable public relations tools for athletes to generate support for their opinions and preferred self-presentations (Sanderson, 2010).

Although many messages protesting media inaccuracies are done indirectly, social media also gives athletes the ability to immediately contact and engage offending journalists. Arizona Cardinals players Darnell Dockett used Twitter to notify sports talk radio host Jim Rome of his disagreement with Rome's commentary. Dockett perceived that Rome was not accurately portraying his Twitter "trash talking" with San Francisco 49ers player Vernon Davis. On May 20, 2010, Dockett tweeted the following:

> "Do yall know twitter is like a mobile Press confrence! Dear Jim Rome, me and @VernonDavis85 are really good friends but thanks for the LUV"
>
> "Can someone Tell JIM ROME I want to go on his show ASAP cause he painting a picture of me and not using all the paint! JIMMY get a me 'BRO'!"

Rome then replied to Dockett via Twitter suggesting that Dockett appear on his radio show:

> "Tv show is booked How about a radio hit tomorrow?"

To which Dockett responded:

> "why radio me when u put me on TV? I want TV time like u had!!!"
> And:
> "@jimrome I want the world to see! Aint that's what u wanted? So let's be fair here!!! TV for TV not TV for Radio."

Rome then replied:

> "@ddockett you're right. How could I "radio" you? I'll get you your tv spot. Standby."

Social media offered Dockett a convenient mechanism to both counter Rome's commentary and advocate for the opportunity to further discuss this situation. Dockett could have arranged this rebuttal via more traditional means (e.g., Cardinals media relations personnel contacting Rome's show to arrange interview), but social media enabled him to instantaneously contact Rome and negotiate to appear via television rather than radio. Cincinnati Bengals wide receiver Chad OchoCinco is another athlete who regularly uses social media to directly confront sports reporters. Prior to the 2009 season, he used Twitter to spar with FoxSports.com journalist Mark Kriegel. Apparently, OchoCinco was upset over critical comments Kriegel made about him. Kriegel had labeled OchoCinco as being indicative of a culture of "chump ballplayers who think they're fabulous and interesting—who believe their personal minutiae has actual merit — despite never having won a thing . . ." (*USA Today*, 2009). OchoCinco responded by tweeting, "Mark Kriegel you're an idiot, you want a Lil fame I'll help, because your story today sucked just like you did in school!!!" and "Mark Kriegel you can come work for me, you're wasting away as a writer for foxsports, from me and my followers you get a 'Child Please!!!'" (Kriegel, 2009a). OchoCinco also has had similar encounters on Twitter with ProFootballTalk.com editor Mike Florio and ESPN NFL analyst Mark Schlereth (*USA Today*, 2009).

Social media will not eliminate sports journalists' criticisms of athletes, but does allow athletes to circulate their disagreements with these media portrayals in a time efficient manner. Additionally, given the large fan followings on both journalists' and athletes' social media sites these debates play out in public forums. Accordingly, sports media personalities may feel pressured to respond to the athlete, as if they ignore the athlete's messages, fans may join the battle by bombarding the media figure with messages on the athlete's behalf. These exchanges may then curb future criticism of the athlete, or at least prompt the journalist to pause and consider if their commentary is worth a confrontation with the athlete.

This trend holds some important implications for the future of sports media. For example, will sports reporters become more guarded in their public critiques of athletes? Will fans who support athletes engage offending journalists on behalf of aggrieved athletes? As athletes can visibly contest perceived framing and inaccuracies, does this compel journalists to exert more diligence in verifying their reports? It is not surprising that conflicts have emerged between athletes and journalists via social media. Sports journalists may resent the increasing media competition from athletes and as a result, continue to condemn athletes for social media use, elevating potential conflicts. Conversely, journalistic "license" may be reined in; prompting sports reporters to be more accountable for their commentary, thereby reducing disagreements and tension between athletes and journalists. As social media and sports media grow more entwined, it is important to discuss some of the broader implications resulting from this merger. The following suggestions represent only a few possible future outcomes. What remains most vital is the recognition that sports media will continue to be influenced and affected by social media. Social media is not going away, formats and platforms will come and go, but the capabilities will only become more pronounced. To that end, it would be prudent for sports media organizations, sports leagues, and sports franchises to diligently monitor social media trends.

Athletes are seizing the opportunity to produce sports media content via social media channels. As a result, sports media consumers have alternative media venues where they can access sports information directly from the source. Thus, as sports media is largely athlete-centric, athletes are poised to draw audiences away from traditional mass media organizations. Moreover, with the interactive capabilities offered by social media channels, fans are no longer solely dependent on sports reporters for news and critique about athletes. Social media shifts sports media into more participative and collaborative formats. In doing so, the line between sports media producers and sports media consumers grows blurry. As the sports media hierarchy grows more diverse and the digital plentitude spreads (Hutchins & Rowe, 2009), traditional sports media organizations are faced with sustainability and survival issues. Scholars have posited that citizen journalism has created a crisis in the news industry (Flew & Wilson, 2010), and this contention also extends to sports media. Although it is difficult to imagine established sports media outlets such as ESPN and *Sports Illustrated* becoming obsolete, as social media requires minimal financial investments, athletes can easily create their own mobile news department. These features place sports media organizations at competitive disadvantages as they have fixed operating costs, employ many people, and yet, are increasingly getting news secondhand after it appears on an athlete's social media site.

In addition to the aforementioned constraints, some sports media organizations and journalists are implementing policies and practices that may hinder their competitive ability. In other words, these entities and individuals are adopting reactive, rather than proactive, responses to the reconfiguration of sports media. For instance, sports media scholars Brad Schultz and Mary Lou Sheffer (2010) conducted a preliminary examination of sports journalists' perceptions of Twitter. They found that established journalists, including print journalists, viewed Twitter as a complementary tool to supplement other reporting, whereas younger journalists perceived Twitter to have transformative capabilities. As the number of print media entities who are folding or contracting in the digital environment, such thinking may be fatal.

Twitter and other social media sites certainly complement sports reporting, but viewing social media in this way, underscores the power of connection and interaction that social media now provide. For example, if I follow Armstrong on Twitter, receive updates from him directly to my cell phone, and send him messages, do I need a sports journalist to keep me informed about him? The degree to which sports media organizations attend to social media bears watching. Sports media organizations are now in competition with both independent media sites *and* athletes. Therefore, sports journalists and sports media organizations should be early adopters of social media technology and consider them as much more than supplementary reporting tools.

Although social media offers a number of strategic benefits to athletes, these advantages can quickly turn problematic. For instance, on August 25, 2009, sports fans learned that NBA player Michael Beasley had checked into a Houston rehabilitation facility (Reynolds, 2009). Several days earlier Beasley had posted a photograph on his Twitter page displaying a new tattoo accompanied with phrases such as "Feelin like it's not worth livin!!!!!!! I'm done," and "I feel like the whole world is against me I can't win for losin" (Kriegel, 2009b). Similarly, in December 2009, reports surfaced that Washington Wizards players Gilbert Arenas and Javaris Crittenton had engaged in a dispute in the locker room, culminating with them pulling guns on each other. This story received comprehensive media attention and in response, Arenas tweeted, "i wake up this morning and seen i was the new JOHN WAYNE. lmao media is too funny." This incident was further exacerbated when Arenas and some of his teammates subsequently demonstrated a mock shooting with their fingers during a pregame warm-up (Corazza, 2010).

These incidents suggest that sports leagues and organizations should take a proactive role in working with athletes to promote strategic social media use. Beasley's tweet clearly suggested that he needed assistance, and he may have been better served by not publicizing these feelings. Although Beasley's tweet was alarming, the ramifications stemming from Arenas' tweet were much more severe. Using Twitter to make light of a very serious situation (as evidenced by Arenas being suspended for the remainder of the 2009-2010 season by NBA commissioner David Stern) placed the Wizards organization in a precarious position with their fans. Could social media training or workshops have prevented these situations? Perhaps. However, considering social media's rapid expansion, devoting time and resources to assist players in managing these media tools may prove beneficial and mitigate public relations issues. Additionally, it would be prudent for social media guidance and instruction to be both comprehensive and consistent and be cautious of the way social media use is framed. For example, if social media is framed negatively, emphasizing disciplinary consequences, with little consideration for athletes' motivations and goals for using these tools, this guidance may prove ineffectual.

Research will play an important role in promoting strategic social media use. For instance, research could measure social media activity (e.g., how many messages per day) message content, objectives in using social media (e.g., connecting with fans, circumventing sports journalists, taking more control over presentation, connecting with other players), and perceptions of social media use (e.g., is it an effective media tool? Is it a distraction?), and what information, if any, is "off limits" for social media? Training could then be developed based on these results. Thus, rather than dwelling on social media prohibitions, sports organizations could explore ways that athletes' social media goals and motivations can be productively achieved.

Although consistent social media training and research would be beneficial with professional athletes, it may be more imperative at the amateur level. There have been several troubling incidents where social media disclosures have created issues for amateur athletes and collegiate athletic programs. One notable incident occurred in July 2010, when the NCAA investigated allegations that University of North Carolina football players Greg Little, Robert Quinn, and Marvin Austin accepted illegal benefits from a sports agent. How NCAA investigators were tipped off offers a cautionary tale for all collegiate athletic programs. In May 2010, Austin posted updates on his Twitter account describing his time in Miami, Florida nightclubs, one of which included, "I live in the club LIV so I get the tenant rate ... bottles comin like it's a giveaway" (Mandel, 2010). In reporting this incident and the subsequent investigation, *Sports Illustrated* college football columnist Stewart Mandel noted:

> the advent of social media—and the inevitable penchant of some young athletes to post incriminating messages or pictures to their Facebook or Twitter accounts—has been a boon to investigators.

and:

> no program with high-profile draft prospects can breathe easily amid the current environment, where new rumors are percolating daily—and one regrettable tweet can send investigators scurrying to your campus.

Although Austin's Twitter account was deactivated, he was dismissed from the team and Little and Quinn were declared permanently ineligible by the NCAA. Mandel's observation about social media being a valuable resource to NCAA investigators is emphasized by many student-athletes maintaining public social media profiles. College students rarely use security settings on social media sites (Peluchette & Karl, 2009), and student-athletes seem to follow their peers in this respect. Thus, the NCAA obtains a free resource that easily is used to monitor potential violations at collegiate athletic programs.

Although the North Carolina case is a shining example, there are plenty of other cases. On February 17, 2010, University of Pittsburgh head football coach Dave Wannstedt dismissed Elijah Fields from the team. Although the coach declined public comment for the rationale behind his decision, Fields' Twitter content was likely the impetus for his removal from the team. Specifically, Fields posted pictures on Twitter depicting large amounts of cash neatly wrapped in rubber bands. As if the pictures alone were not sufficiently incriminating, Fields added the following descriptors for the photographs, "More to Come and Its Mine BITCH Burrr," and "Never knew Football was gon get me all this money Sike I knew haha" (HuffingtonPost.com, 2010).

On January 16, 2010, three football recruits who were on an official visit to Mississippi State University, posted Facebook status updates referencing the "Pony," a designation for a local gentleman's club (Staples, 2010). The recruits indicated that their references were meant in jest; nevertheless, Mississippi State launched an investigation. This response was not surprising given the strict NCAA guidelines governing athletic recruiting and the problematic behavior that has occurred during these visits (e.g., in 2004, University of Colorado football players invited female strippers to a recruiting party). This revelation came on the heels of a 2009 incident involving University of Florida football recruits Leon Orr and Lynden Trail. In this case, a blogger retrieved pictures from these two players' MySpace profiles and then posted them online, where they were quickly picked up by Deadspin, greatly increasing their public visibility. The photographs depicted Orr grasping a pistol in his right hand and holding $16 in his other hand, while Trail was displayed wearing a bandana, making what was presumed to be a gang sign with his fingers (Staples, 2009). Interestingly, both photographs were taken when these individuals were in the eighth grade, several years before they began to be recruited. Both players acknowledged that they had planned to "clean up" their profiles, but had not yet completed this task.

These examples suggest that amateur athletes should be mindful when posting social media content. These incidents reflect current concerns surrounding college students posting controversial content on social media profiles, that is then accessed by potential employers (Elzweig & Peeples, 2009; Peluchette & Karl, 2009). Research also indicates that younger people are not aware of social media privacy settings or simply choose to ignore them (Debatin, Lovejoy, Horn, & Hughes, 2009; Taraszow, Aristodemou, Shitta, Laouris, & Arsoy, 2010). Although organizational monitoring of social media is discussed more explicitly in a later chapter, it would be advisable for collegiate athletic programs and perhaps even high schools to adopt social media training as part of an orientation curriculum. These efforts may prevent social media pitfalls, mitigate disciplinary consequences such as the revocation of athletic eligibility, and promote strategic social media habits that stay with them throughout their athletic career.

In conclusion, social media will only grow further entrenched in the sports media landscape. Social media offers athletes unique media production opportunities that are extremely valuable in contesting media inaccuracies and forming relationships with fans. Athletes now exert more control over their public representation and manage these images in alternative media venues that are easily accessible to audience members. Conversely, social media content also produces public relations issues, suggesting that athletes and sports organizations must be diligent in managing these media tools. Additionally, the outcomes resulting from this sports media shift may extend well beyond content and access—there are serious financial implications. If fans continue to gravitate to athletes' social media sites, athletes can market these audiences to advertisers (some already have), providing additional revenue streams and offering sponsors additional venues to market their products.

The digital sports media environment is complex (Rowe, 2004) and has created a multitude of challenges for, among others, athletes, sports media entities, sports organizations, and collegiate athletic programs. How social media continues to integrate into the sports media environment may well influence societal perceptions about the marriage of these two media formats. For instance, social media may soon be perceived to be on par with newspapers, television stations, or magazines, leading audiences to view news on released via these channels to be as credible as the newspaper or sportscast. T. Miller (2009) coined the term "Media 3.0" (p. 6) to characterize media studies that are shaped by collective identity and group experiences of social spaces. Athletes' social media sites are functioning as spaces where collective identity is expressed as fans and athletes cooperatively produce and interpret sports media. Thus, social media populates what was once a restricted and tightly controlled sphere with media venues that limit the monopolizing forces of traditional sports media.

3

SOCIAL MEDIA AND SPORTS
ORGANIZATIONAL IMPLICATIONS

There are multiple ways that organizations are incorporating social media into their business models. For instance, they use social media to expand their marketing capabilities (e.g., a sandwich shop that "tweets" daily specials to customers) and to perform public relations (e.g., General Motors using the "Faces of GM" employee blogs to rebuild public confidence after their financial bailout by the U.S. government). Although these efforts are certainly noteworthy and have been adopted by many sports organizations, this chapter is concerned with issues arising from athletes and team personnel using social media. Sports organizations, similar to their counterparts in other employment sectors, are grappling with managing social media.

Social media have created a number of challenges for organizations, particularly with managing information. Information control is a legitimate organizational concern to protect confidential data. For example, if trade secrets were disclosed, the organization's competitive sustainability could be compromised. Moreover, if personnel information was released, the organization could face litigation. Although the potential for employees to release confidential information always has been an organizational worry, social media significantly expands the opportunity for sensitive information to be revealed. Social media messages can be transmitted from any location where a person has Internet access, extending the possibility for information breaches well beyond the physical confines of the workplace. Accordingly, organizations now face greater difficulty in controlling information release, and in some cases, may not learn this has occurred until the disclosure is reported in the media. Although organizations do enact consequences toward those who reveal private information (e.g., termination of employment), they still must expend significant resources to quell the unanticipated publicity created by such disclosures.

Although social media hinders an organization's ability to control information, it correspondingly increases the organization's ability to monitor both current and prospective employees. In some cases, workers are unaware that their employer is viewing their social media profiles until being disciplined for the content on these sites (Genova, 2009). Organizational access to social media profiles is easily achieved as most people fail to completely or fully use privacy settings (Debatin et al., 2009; Taraszow et al., 2010). This capability has become an extremely popular employer practice and not surprisingly, has prompted a number of questions about privacy. For instance, where are the boundaries between "personal" and "work?" To what extent should employers discipline employees for social media content? Should employers access the social media profiles of applicants and factor content into hiring decisions? Social media has become a very "hot" topic in employment law (Salter & Bryden, 2009) and the sports world offers a number of compelling examples that typify the contemporary issues surrounding social media and the workplace.

Whereas employees in other industries rarely attract public attention for their social media disclosures, messages from athletes, team employees, and sports figures receive much more notoriety. Although connecting with athletes and sports figures is a compelling outcome that social media has introduced, it is easy to forget that athletes are employees, and that sports organizations and sports leagues are *employers*. Thus, just as other employers monitor and discipline employees for social media issues, sports organizations are following suit. Sports organizations historically have been very guarded in controlling information and stifling dissent (e.g., fines levied on athletes and team personnel for criticizing officiating), a task that social media greatly complicates. Sports organizations do enact consequences toward those who violate social media policies, but these sanctions come after the issue has occurred. Given the maelstrom of publicity that certain disclosures create, assertively working to mitigate issues will prevent sports organizations having to hurriedly enact responses to divert intense press and public attention.

One of the more notable cases involving an athlete revealing information without the organization's knowledge occurred with Minnesota Timberwolves player Kevin Love. On June 16, 2009, Love disclosed via

Twitter that head coach Kevin McHale had been fired by the organization, "Today is a sad day … Kevin McHale will NOT be back as head coach this season." Once this disclosure went public, mass media organizations quickly bombarded the Timberwolves with questions, as McHale's departure had not been formally announced. Within an hour after this posting, Love tweeted, "I am not a news-breaking guy … I had no idea no one knew … I'll tell them I stayed at a holiday inn express last night" (Associated Press, 2009d). Although the Timberwolves initially declined to confirm McHale's dismissal—that was the ultimate outcome. Love clearly had insider information about McHale's situation which he then broadcasted, catching the Timberwolves off guard. Love also used Twitter to post skeptical commentary about the Timberwolves selecting two point guards, Ricky Rubio and Jonny Flynn, with consecutive picks during the 2009 NBA Draft, by asking "What are we doing?" (Knott, 2009).

It is plausible that the Timberwolves were dismayed with Love for disclosing confidential information and broadcasting what appeared to be critical commentary about personnel decisions. Sports organizations are paying closer attention to athlete's social media content, and in some cases, publicizing requests for the athlete to modify their social media behavior (as the Florida Marlins did in June 2011 with outfielder Logan Morrison). Sports organizations certainly have a reasonable expectation that confidential information will not be publicly shared. To some extent, however, this has been occurring for years, through "anonymous" sources "leaking" stories to the media. Social media introduce more complexity however, as commentary posted via these networks provides a record of the message, making it more difficult to plausibly deny statements. Social media provides a written record that documents the time the messages was shared and is linked to an identifiable spokesperson.

To prevent social media issues, some sports organizations restrict players from using these tools altogether. Although this may seem a plausible way to prevent future problems, athletes may be reluctant to give up these media tools, and such directives may then incite conflict. Additionally, social media can be used for "whistle-blowing," giving athletes a convenient way to report harassment or bullying by coaches or other team personnel, reports that can be bolstered through photographs and audio recordings. Prohibiting social media may then prevent athletes from reporting hostile working conditions and silences an important outlet through which these concerns can be raised.

Although banning social media use can be considered a restrictive approach, other sports organizations have adopted policies to govern its use. However, these policies often are more concerned with time, rather than content restrictions. For instance, the NFL's social media policy restricts players from using social media starting 90 minutes before a game, during the game, and lasting through the end of postgame media interviews

(Associated Press, 2009f; Stradley, 2009). Similarly, the NBA prohibits players and coaches from using cell phones and other electronic communication devices starting 45 minutes prior to a game, during the game, and lasting until the completion of postgame media obligations. However, some NBA teams, including the Miami Heat, Toronto Raptors, Milwaukee Bucks, and Los Angeles Clippers, have adopted policies that restrict players' from using social media during anything classified as "team time." A former Clippers head coach explained the scope of this policy by commenting, "The minute you're on our property, there's no tweeting" (Stein, 2009).

These policies also have trickled down to collegiate athletic programs. On May 11, 2010, University of Georgia basketball player Trey Thompkins tweeted, "Don't expect anymore interesting tweets from me. ... Don't ask me why, but there will be NONE ANYMORE!!!" Head coach Mark Fox provided the following rationale for the decision to restrict players from using Twitter, "I want our players to focus on our team, I don't want to hear a bunch of Tweets, It's about going into the offseason and getting better" (SI.com, 2010). Although social media policies and fines for violating these policies may deter some athletes and sports figures from using social media, they may be inconsequential for others. For example, NBA owner Mark Cuban indicated that the NBA's social media policy would not hinder his Twitter use. Cuban's reaction was not especially surprising, considering that he has been fined on multiple occasions for criticizing NBA officiating on his blog and Twitter (Stein, 2009). Thus, some athletes and sports figures consider the fines and disciplinary action that accompany their social media use to be worth the cost.

Sports organizations certainly are within their bounds to implement social media policies. However, only regulating the time frames when social media can be used but offering little clarification about content may account for the incongruent perceptions between athletes and sports organizations. With little content guidance, when athletes begin posting messages that violate organizational boundaries, athletes are disciplined or admonished to cease their social media activity. Organizational expectations may be covered with athletes, but given the frequency with which social media missteps occur, it may be prudent to consistently negotiate clear boundaries that govern acceptable social media use. This will be particularly important as social media channels progress and communicative capabilities increase.

Existing policies, although perhaps effective in limiting in-game revelations, seem to have minimal effect in reducing problematic social media disclosures. Additionally, highly restrictive polices seem likely to elevate conflict between sports organizations and athletes. Research suggests that employees react negatively when they perceive that employers are intrusively monitoring their communication (Snyder & Cornetto, 2009). These conflicting views also may prompt employees to circumvent employers

(Kassing, 2007) and publicize the employer's practices across social media networks. In doing so, they both increase the visibility of these policies and invite public support, an approach many athletes and sports figures are using as they wrestle with sports organizations over social media.

For instance, on August 4, 2009, the San Diego Chargers fined corner-back Antonio Cromartie $2,500 after he tweeted about the "nasty food" being served in the team's training camp cafeteria. Cromartie also insinuated that the substandard culinary options may have contributed to the team's postseason troubles. This comment violated a directive issued by Chargers head coach Norv Turner who had informed players that they were not to tweet while in team buildings or tweet critical information about the team (Associated Press, 2009e). Despite this sanction, Cromartie indicated that he would continue tweeting, and notified his Twitter followers, "wld like to think all my new followers since I got fine I promise I wnt let u down ok look forward to sum grt stuff 2 come." However, he did acknowledge that he would be more cautious about future postings, "man we had a grt practice 2day The defense flow around we made a lot of plays every1 knows I have 2 watch wht i say now cause i got fined" (Associated Press, 2009e).

Interestingly, several NFL players publicly defended Cromartie's tweet. In different ways, these colleagues argued that players should be able to express their opinions without retribution being taken. Teammate Shawne Merriman elected to joke about the incident by tweeting:

> lets make a deal if all yall pitch in a dollar ill tweet more they handing out fines like free turkeys on thanksgiving, ya dig?, you can be tough alllllll you want to but the first time you get hit for a $2500 fine my name goes from LightsOut to just switch lol. ... And by the way i thought the food was AMAZING today haha yea im a suck up. (Associated Press, 2009e)

Terrell Owens (then with the Buffalo Bills) opined, "I think it's ridiculous. For someone to get fined $2,500 because they tweeted that the cafeteria food was bad ... then maybe they need to change (the food). That's his honest opinion" (*Toronto Sun*, 2009). Buffalo Bills linebacker Kavika Mitchell was terser in his response, posted via Twitter:

> Our voice is our rite. It's bullsh!t that the league is scared of twitter. We have opinions. We sit back ... and listen to all the bullsh!t media, coaches and fans have to say, so if the chargers food sucks. It sucks. Please! B mad at real sh!t. (Sports Business Daily, 2009)

Cromartie was subsequently traded by the Chargers to the New York Jets in March 2010. Although this transaction was largely attributed to Cromartie's private problems involving paternity issues, some press accounts seamlessly inserted Cromartie's cafeteria food critique when discussing his off-the field issues (Cimini, 2010). Cromartie's comments clearly upset the Chargers and although it is unclear whether using Twitter played a role in his trade to the Jets, it suggests that teams may elect to move players who post negative commentary about the team. It certainly is understandable that sports organizations want to mitigate public criticism; however, it may be prudent for them to strategically determine which battles they will fight. In this case, the discipline enacted toward Cromartie fueled public support from other players and created more media attention than the Chargers would have preferred. Had the Chargers ignored this commentary or addressed their concerns with Cromartie without fining him, less attention may have resulted. Additionally, although polices do have their merit, this incident suggests that each offense may need to be evaluated separately, to determine if enacting discipline may be more detrimental than handling the issue without discipline.

Clearly, the rate with which athletes have adopted social media has forced sports organizations to quickly determine how to best manage these media tools. Some organizations may draft and enforce policies with the expectation that social media is a temporary fad. However, athletes and social media are a permanent, not a temporary marriage, and therefore, it will be important to undertake collaborative approaches to manage social media. This may require sports organizations to accept that there will be occasional disclosures that are frustrating but which do not warrant corrective action. Instead, sports organizations may need to outline specific types of content that is prohibited (e.g., no commentary on pending personnel moves) and clarify expectations (Does criticism of the team extend to meal selections?).

Additionally, it is possible that stringent policies may actually increase, rather than decrease, social media issues for sports organizations. It is reasonable to expect athletes to refrain from using social media during competition, yet it appears there needs to be more negotiating about social media use outside these time frames. For example, extending social media restrictions to encompass anytime an athlete is on "team property" or prohibiting use of these sites entirely seems likely to fuel dissent and dissatisfaction. Sports organizations also should be cautious about the ways they frame social media use. There is a tendency for sports organizations (and sports journalists) to frame athletes' social media use as a "distraction," suggesting that using social media and being a team player are incongruent. Couching social media use in these terms positions athletes as being incapable of balancing social media with their athletic careers. However, many athletes do use social media responsibly and thus it may be hasty to presume that these tools detract from team chemistry. Sports organizations may benefit from distinguishing between the strengths and weaknesses that social media offers, and work in concert with athletes to maximize positive outcomes. Such approaches may promote more harmony between sports organizations and athletes, moving away from the conflict that appears to be dominating this issue.

The conflicts emanating from social media use by athletes and sports figures are largely rooted in issues of information control. With social media, athletes are becoming more active media producers, a capability that brings both advantages and risks. The public format of many social media sites allows organizations to monitor what athletes are saying (often away from the workplace) and disciplining them accordingly. These actions mirror prevailing workplace-monitoring trends. That is, social media sites are a cost-effective way to keep tabs on workers (Jourdan, 2010; Petrecca, 2010; *USA Today*, 2010). Thus, sports organizations find themselves locked in competition with athletes over information ownership. Social media has greatly influenced this struggle by widening the ability for athletes to disclose information outside of the organization's control.

SOCIAL MEDIA AND INFORMATION CONTROL

Sports organizations must protect proprietary data that could negatively impact them if publicly released. For instance, if an athlete were to reveal play calls, it would create an extreme disadvantage during athletic play. Additionally, if the organization's anticipated personnel movements were revealed, other franchises could counter these moves, producing unforeseen setbacks in personnel strategy. At a broader level, with the prominence of sports gambling, sports leagues have a genuine concern about information being released that could influence gambling lines, potentially threatening perceptions of the league's integrity. Sports organizations have always been faced with such concerns and must now attend to social media as viable avenues for information leaks. Social media inhibits the control sports organizations maintain over information. In the past, although confidential information could be revealed, these disclosures often were made to reporters. In some cases, relationships between sports organizations and sports journalists are predicated on tacit understandings when these situations occur. In other words, if certain information was disclosed, reporters would not release it or would at least delay reporting it. Teams also can limit media availability of athletes whom they consider likely to disclose sensitive information. As social media can be accessed outside the organization's control, athletes are now volunteering unsolicited information, making it difficult to manage information release.

Moreover, it is harder for sports organizations to control and rectify the consequences when these situations occur. Athletes' social media messages have large public reach, extending nationally and in some cases, globally, and content can be transmitted from a variety of locations using a host of technological devices. Thus, an athlete could be well beyond the geographical proximity of the organization when disclosing this information. There is simply no feasible way for sports organizations to monitor every potential social media avenue by which an athlete could reveal confidential information. Additionally, when problematic messages are disseminated, it is difficult for the organization to "clean up" the message and pacify mass media attention. For example, if an athlete releases information during a press interview, sports organizations can suggest that comments were taken out of context, particularly if the athlete is just finishing a game. Attributions can be perpetuated that the athlete was dealing with the emotional exhilaration and therefore, not properly composed to offer commentary.

When these incidents occur on social media sites, it is more difficult to downplay commentary as the athlete is offering the information willingly and has had ample time to construct the message. These outcomes, however, do not hinder sports organizations from instituting damage control, when they perceive that problematic social media content has been issued. For example, one mechanism that is employed is sending a message clarifying an earlier post, often within a short duration after the initial message is released. Such an event occurred on July 30, 2009, when Minnesota Vikings player Visanthe Shiancoe tweeted, "Zzzzzz zzzz zzzz zzz (in meetings) lol. Introducing the staff." This tweet was promptly followed by a clarifying tweet, "My earlier tweet with the 'zzzzzzzz's' was concerning an administrative meeting and not a team meeting" (Darnell, 2009).

Although athletes in many sports have generated social media controversy, NFL players have been at the forefront. Accordingly, the league is visibly concerned about the propensity of players to divulge private information via social media (Maese, 2009). To alleviate these concerns, the NFL monitors the Twitter use of its players (J. Miller, 2010), and as part of its social media policy, the league bans players from using mobile devices in bench areas. This directive may have been issued in response to OchoCinco, who adamantly expressed that he would tweet from the sidelines during a game. Naturally, when this policy was announced, OchoCinco was upset and aired his grievances on Twitter. Specifically, "Damn NFL and these rules, I am going by my own set of rules, I ain't hurting nobody or getting in trouble, I am putting my foot down!!" (Maese, 2009). Not to be denied, OchoCinco then announced that he would hold a weekly contest on Twitter where fans could help him circumvent this policy. He planned to fly a fan in for each Bengals home game and then using hand signals, communicate messages to that person, who would then tweet for him. However, the NFL quickly responded to this counter-move and amended their policy to prohibit social media use during athletic contests by players or *anyone representing them* (Parr, 2009, italics added).

Although the NFL has been able to prevent players from using social media during games, this is not true for the NBA. On March 15, 2009, Milwaukee Bucks player Charlie Villanueva tweeted during halftime of a game against the Boston Celtics, "In da locker room, snuck to post my twitt. We're playing the Celtics, tie ball game at da half. Coach wants more toughness. I gotta step up." When Bucks coach Scott Skiles found out what Villanueva had done, he was unhappy. In speaking to the media, Skiles stated, "We made a point to Charlie and the team that it's nothing we ever want to happen again." Villanueva agreed to cease posting during games, but did take the issue up with his Twitter followers, "I'm looking for some answers here, what's the difference between halftime twitting and halftime interview?" (Bierman & Hoffman, 2009, p. 10). At the time of Villanueva's posting, the NBA did not have a social media policy, but one appeared very quickly thereafter (Stein, 2009).

Further complicating this issue for sports organizations is that athletes are not the only team employees who might reveal information via social media. On May 21, 2010, Myron Goodman, a sales representative for the Washington Wizards used Facebook to announce the team's plans for the first overall pick in the 2010 NBA Draft. Goodman posted a message on a Facebook page for University of Kentucky alumni stating that the Wizards would be selecting former University of Kentucky player John Wall. The message declared, "I am a sales rep for the Washington Wizards. John Wall will be our choice as the (No. 1) overall pick in the June draft. If you want a great deal in tickets . . . email me." Naturally, it did not take long for this news to spread, for the posting to be deleted, and for Wizards spokesman Scott Hall to issue a public statement. The official statement framed Goodman's actions as "an overzealous member of our sales staff acting on his own" (Associated Press, 2010d).

The Wizards ultimately selected Wall with the first overall pick in the Draft. Although the Wizards were vague with the public about its intentions, it seems plausible that the organization may have informed certain internal employees about selecting Wall. Such information could be strategically used by certain team employees to prepare marketing and public relations campaigns that would be prepared to launch once Wall was selected. The Wizards clearly did not want their intentions publicized, and when this information leaked, they had to invest time and effort to address the media attention created by the incident. Additionally, although speculation of the Wizards' intentions circulated across the Internet, Goodman's Facebook profile was easily identifiable. This left little room for the Wizards to issue a denial, thus, Goodman was conveniently framed as too eager in performing his job duties.

The public relations dilemmas that social media creates for sports organizations also stem from the ability of users to construct and broadcast messages with little filtering. As such, inappropriate self-disclosures are becoming commonplace across social media forums. Although some people may perceive that their commentary is confidential, unless privacy settings are configured to limit public viewing, these messages are easily accessible (Peluchette & Karl, 2009; Qian & Scott, 2007). Athletes and sports figures certainly are not the only group affected by this social media outcome. However, with their high public profiles and large followings, questionable social media content quickly spreads and becomes heavily publicized.

SOCIAL MEDIA AND SELF-DISCLOSURE

Problematic social media disclosures emanating from athletes provide a lightning rod for media coverage. Thus, when these incidents do occur, sports organizations are compelled to initiate public relations responses. These announcements increasingly involve pronouncements that the athlete has received guidance about social media use. Yet, despite this counsel and the media attention and controversy generated by these messages, they continue to manifest. Covering every incident is well beyond the scope of this book, but some of the more prominent cases are now profiled.

Social media has greatly enhanced the ability for fans and athletes to connect, and although these exchanges can be positive, they also are ripe for conflict. One of the more telling examples of such behavior occurred on October 25, 2009, and involved then Kansas City Chiefs running back Larry Johnson. After a loss against the San Diego Chargers, Johnson turned to Twitter to voice his displeasure with head coach Todd Haley, "my father got more credentials than most of these pro coaches ... google my father!!!!!!!" Then "My father played for the coach from 'rememeber the titans.' Our coach played golf. My father played for redskins briefley. Our coach. Nuthn" (Van Grove, 2009). One person responded to these criticisms by tweeting, "Interesting comments by Larry Johnson (@toonlcon) about 'coaches.' Hey LJ, is it Haley's fault you fall when D-Linemen blow on you?" Another tweet soon followed that referenced Johnson's previous domestic allegations, "Apologies. His Twitter alias is @toonicon whatever the hell that means. Probably something about spitting in women's faces" (Van Grove, 2009).

The proverbial floodgates then opened and others began condemning Johnson. Johnson apparently reached his limit and launched a barrage of tweets in response to his attackers:

> "Make me regret it. Lmao. U don't stop my checks. Lmao. So 'tweet' away."
>
> "@[Lists Twitter ID] then don't reply then. Still richer then u. Keep goin. Come play our game ooops forgot u can't."
>
> "@[Lists Twitter ID] got nuthn to do wit hiring my father. But u wouldn't know cuz u don't play either so keep on the sideline lil gril n cheer."
>
> "@[Lists Twitter ID] sorry to tell u ur the reason y ur broke n dissn on twitter lmao."
>
> "@[Lists Twitter ID] think bout a clever diss then wit ur fag pic. Christopher street boy. Is what us east coast cats call u."
>
> "@[Lists Twitter ID] Sorry ur a cornball n ur mom birthed u broke. But I'm cakn patna. While u work or school for 5 dollas n hour. Ha!"

The next day reporters questioned Johnson about his tweet, and he refused to back off his comments. Based on these actions, the Chiefs suspended him for 2 weeks for "conduct detrimental to the team" a disciplinary action that cost him almost $300,000 (Battista, 2009b). On November 9, 2009, the Chiefs released Johnson, and he eventually signed with the Cincinnati Bengals. Johnson's social media commentary had serious financial repercussions and seemed to play a role in the Chiefs severing their employment relationship with him. Despite the severe consequences suffered by Johnson as result of this social media confrontation, it was only a few short months later that the Santonio Holmes incident occurred.

Athletes and fans engaging in hostile verbalizations toward one another is not a new phenomenon. However, these exchanges generally take place within the confines of athletic stadiums and typically are dissipated before becoming problematic. Additionally, with the high levels of security at sporting venues, coupled with the distance between players and spectators (which admittedly varies by sport), the potential to engage athletes is limited to those in close proximity to the action. Social media, however, enables fans to voice criticisms directly to athletes, which some players take personally. They then reciprocate with their own aggressive communication and these exchanges play out in a public forum, almost certainly guaranteeing that these actions will hit the newswire. Additionally, when confrontation between athletes and fans happens within the confines of the stadium, these incidents generally end with little afterthought. Each of these actors can plausibly deny allegations about their hostilities, and given the loud noise present in stadiums, attempts to record commentary on a cellular phone or other digital device may prove difficult. With social media, written records of messages are easily retrievable and can quickly be transmitted across the Internet. This ensures high visibility will be obtained, even if athletes delete these messages from their social media profile.

Although athletes are no strangers to taunting from fans, when these episodes move from physical to virtual spheres, problems are bound to escalate. It is reasonable to expect athletes to defend themselves against attacks posted to their social media profiles. Yet, given the financial repercussions that can result, rather than responding to these individuals, they may be better served deleting offensive commentary and blocking these people from participating on their profile. Another potential step is to publicize the commentary posted by such individuals. LeBron James, who has been the subject of considerable criticism for his free agency departure from the Cleveland Cavaliers to the Miami Heat, used Twitter in this manner. James posted a tweet that encouraged fans to "hate" on him. James then publicly posted some of the more egregious tweets he received, including those filled with derogatory racial terms. James certainly could have engaged these individuals, but by taking the "higher road," he strategically exposed these individuals and their disconcerting commentary.

These incidents suggest that sports organizations, players associations, agents, and collegiate athletic programs, may need to work with athletes to develop strategies that can be employed to respond to critiques directed via social media. Potential topics that could be covered in such discussions include the permanence of social media messages, the financial ramifications, and the potential to be released or traded. It also would be worthwhile to ensure that athletes know how to use privacy settings and to block hostile people from participating on their profile.

Closely related to this topic is the need for players to be cautioned about mobile technology. Two examples from the NBA forcefully drive this point home. On January 27, 2010, Portland Trailblazers player Greg Oden issued a public apology after nude pictures of him appeared on the Internet (Associated Press, 2010a). Oden acknowledged that in 2008, he had taken the pictures on his cell phone and sent them to an ex-girlfriend. A little over a week later, on February 9, 2010, San Antonio Spurs player George Hill issued a public apology after nude pictures he had taken of himself also ended up online (Associated Press, 2010b). The motivation behind these actions is uncertain, but also beside the issue. Oden and Hill may have had little reason to believe that these pictures would ever become public, yet cell phone photographs are easily stored and uploaded to enable wide distribution. Although instructing athletes to avoid taking and sending nude pictures may be considered intrusive and restrictive, never having to address this issue may be worth the sacrifice.

Aggressive communication displays toward fans are but one type of disclosure that leads to public relations issues for sports organizations. The propensity for athletes to disclose intimate details about private activities also creates controversy. One of the more interesting ways this has manifested is by athletes using social media to coordinate liaisons with women while traveling. Kansas City Chiefs wide receiver Dwayne Bowe created a stir when he disclosed to *ESPN The Magazine* that teammates were using Facebook and Twitter to contact and schedule women to rendezvous with while on road trips (Matz, 2010). As if this tidbit from Bowe was not sufficient, another article in this same magazine issue asked various athletes about items they brought with them on the road to make travel more bearable. In describing why condoms were his essential road item, surfer Jamie Sterling declared:

> I'm not the only athlete who believes in safe sex, but I'm the most prepared. I bring condoms according to the length of my stay, but on average, I have 12 on me at all times, just in case. Four or five for me, the rest for friends. When your buddies are unprepared, and you hook them up with the condom that seals their deal, it makes you feel pretty good. (Alipour, 2010, p. 100)

Another news story profiled how an Australian woman used Facebook to connect women with football players to coordinate sex (Pandaram, 2009). Although the groupie culture has been prominent in sports for some time, social media now expands the ability for athletes to coordinate these liaison, and facilitate practices such as importing. However, although the groupie culture is understood to exist, it seems plausible that sports organizations would prefer that these details not be publicized. Chiefs head coach Todd Haley indicated as much in discussing his meeting with Bowe after the unexpected publicity generated by his comments:

> Dwayne and I had a long conversation and from this point on, we'll leave it at that, that it was discussed, handled internally and we're moving forward. We're worried about making progress as a team as we go forward and that's what's really important to me now. (ESPN.com, 2010b)

To what extent sports organizations know that practices such as importing groupies are occurring and discussed with players is uncertain. These incidents suggest that if these social media practices were not previously covered, they will be in future sessions.

There are several important reasons for sports organizations to investigate if these practices are occurring in their organization. First, fraternizing

with groupies is risky because it can prompt allegations of sexual misconduct against athletes, incidents that are not in short supply. Considering the
legal and media ramifications that result when an athlete is accused of sexual impropriety, taking every possible preventative measure seems worth the
investment. Second, it does not take long to browse the list of followers on
many athletes' social media profiles to reasonably conclude that some of
these people are not interested in sports news. Many of these individuals
post provocative message and photographs to the athlete, which may facilitate contact. Some of these followers may have malicious designs, and athletes should be cautioned about meeting up with strangers, as these liaisons
could potentially ruin their careers. In working with athletes to mitigate the
potential for sexual misconduct, sports organizations and other vested parties (e.g., players associations, agents) may want to encourage athletes to be
selective in whom they allow to participate on their social media profiles.
Inherently, this is a restrictive measure, but if such action prevents even one
incident of sexual abuse or rape, reducing social media connections may be
worthwhile.

A third reason to be proactive in attending to these practices is that
intimate details of these events are easily publicized. Many of these women
are chronicling their exploits with athletes on their own social media profiles, broadcasting what is presumed to be a private encounter for public
consumption. Once these events are transmitted, audiences flock to sites
where they can learn about the intimate details of these dalliances and a
public relations issue is born. Moreover, given the intensity with which
celebrity-news–driven sites such as TMZ.com seek gossip about celebrities,
social media are fertile ground to obtain such information. Once this
occurs, sports organizations and athletes are immediately bombarded with
media attention that necessitates a response, which often involves assur-
ances that the athlete has been spoken to—but little else. When these events
occur, it may be beneficial to disclose what corrective action is being taken,
information that may reduce future occurrences. Additionally, by disseminating plans to prevent future incidents (e.g., training for players about
these incidents), sports organizations offer the public a tangible action plan
that also may assist other sports organizations in addressing these issues
with their players.

Social media clearly has created a host of issues for sports organizations
with respect to managing information. Considering that it is impractical for
sports organizations to regulate every possible social media avenue, it may
be advisable for them to categorize social media risk levels. For instance, if
it becomes public that the team's cafeteria food is not desirable, this is
much less worrisome than players posting derogatory or homophobic messages. In coming to such decisions, it seems prudent for sports organizations to collaborate with athletes and players associations. Adopting such

an approach will create a social media partnership that may help minimize problematic social media occurrences.

Using collective frameworks for social media management also may reduce use of these tools by athletes and sports figures to express their frustration with sports organizations. Social media offers these individuals highly visible forums to voice dissent. Accordingly, highly restrictive and unilateral social media policies and management may drive athletes to circumvent these policies and openly flaunt this activity across social media networks. As social media provides athletes and sports figures with access to empathetic, supportive audiences, their grievances may generate fan support, thereby pressuring the sports organization.

SOCIAL MEDIA AND DISSENT

When employees experience incongruence with workplace policies and practices, they voice these feelings by expressing dissent (Kassing, 1997). In conveying these concerns, employees select from three different audiences by (a) dissenting upwardly to their supervisor; (b) dissenting laterally to co-workers; or (c) enacting displaced dissent by sharing their feelings with family members, friends, or others outside the organization (Kassing, 1997, 1998; Kassing & DiCioccio, 2004). Although athletes and sports figures do enact upward and lateral dissent, social media has greatly enhanced the ability to engage in displaced dissent. With social media, athletes and sports figures have access to diverse audience groups. As such, these domains provide valuable spaces where dissent can be broadcast and support can be fostered with audience members. Certainly, there are risks involved when expressing dissent as sports organizations consistently fine those who publicize their dissatisfaction. Despite these sanctions, social media is growing more prominent as a forum for athletes and sports figures to convey their displeasure and frustration with sports organizations.

Dallas Mavericks owner Mark Cuban is one of the most visible sports figures using social media to express dissent. Since purchasing the Mavericks franchise in 2000, Cuban has consistently voiced his displeasure with the NBA's officiating. In January 2002, Cuban stated that Ed Rush, head of NBA officials at the time, was not qualified to work at a Dairy Queen. This commentary resulted in a $500,000 fine from NBA commissioner David Stern (Cuaycong, 2002). On another occasion, in June 2006, after the Mavericks lost an NBA finals game against the Miami Heat, Cuban rushed to the floor and began launching profanities at officials. Cuban then turned to Stern and declared, "--- you! ---! Your league is rigged!" (Isola, 2006, p. 61). This action netted Cuban a $250,000 fine.

In addition to these critiques, Cuban uses his blog and Twitter account as additional venues to express dissent. In May 2006, Cuban was fined $200,000 after posting a blog entry suggesting that the NBA needed to stop rewarding officials with playoff assignments (Soshnick, 2006). In March 2009, Cuban was fined $25,000 after tweeting his displeasure with NBA officials failing to discipline Denver Nuggets player J.R. Smith for taunting Mavericks player Antoine Wright during a game. Cuban responded to this fine by tweeting, "can't say no one makes money from twitter. the NBA does" (Associated Press, 2009a).

Cuban is far from the only critic of NBA officiating. Many players, coaches, and team personnel members regularly are fined for expressing their frustration with officiating. Whereas some of these criticisms are products of emotional feelings following games, with social media, athletes and sports figures can construct meaningful dissent messages. These postings allow them to elaborate on the rationale behind their displeasure and supplement their arguments with evidence. For example, in Sanderson (2009b), I observed that Cuban's blog postings backed up his grievances with factual evidence and provided solutions to officiating problems, which fostered support for his dissent from blog readers. These strategies have been conceptualized in dissent research as direct-factual appeals and solution presentation (Kassing, 2002), highly competent dissent strategies (Kassing, 2005). In Sanderson (2009b), I argued that using these strategies enabled Cuban to cultivate dissent among his blog readers. These audience members expressed gratitude and support for Cuban's efforts to improve officiating, which encouraged and reinforced his dissent, despite the financial sanctions they produced. Although Cuban may not have been seeking validation for his dissent, his blog became a public space where fans could express frustration with the league and rally behind a figure who visibly represented their concerns.

Orlando Magic player Dwight Howard also has used his blog to voice frustration with NBA officiating. During the Magic's 2010 first-round series against the Charlotte Bobcats, Howard was highly ineffective because of fouls. After the Magic won the series, he blogged that the games against the Bobcats represented the "most frustrating stretch of my career." He then suggested that officials were not affording him the same treatment that other star players received. Howard indicated that he did not see "other star players getting called for fouls the way I get them. No star player in the league is outta games the way I am." The NBA promptly fined Howard $35,000 for these critiques (Landman, 2010). In November 2009, Howard also was fined $15,000 for lambasting officials on his blog after the Magic lost to the Detroit Pistons:

I was on the floor for 16 minutes and fouled out!!! Let me say that
again: 17 minutes and six fouls!!! How can that be, y'all? It was crazy.
They called me for a charge on a flop, a push off when the defender was
on me and two fouls on blocked shots. . . . They are letting guys ham-
mer me one end of the floor, yet I'm being called for everything.
(Zillgitt & Colston, 2009, p. 10C)

Although sports organizations seek to curb criticism about officiating,
social media presents challenges. First, complaints about officiating are a
commonality shared by athletes, sports figures, and fans. In using social
media to voice concerns with officiating, these grievances are aired in sympathetic environments that prompt fans to reciprocate, encouraging athletes
and sports figures to continue expressing dissent about this issue. Second, a
verbal tirade about officiating after a game may be dismissed easily or viewed
as insignificant, but using social media bolsters dissent claims. For example,
athletes and sports figures can support their claims with evidence and present solutions to the problem. Thus, rather than dismissing these dissent
expressions as "complaining" or "whining," supplementing them with compelling evidence and practical solutions helps them gain more credibility.

Sports leagues do invest resources to monitor officiating and rectify
inadequacies. Officiating perceptions are subjective and solutions are
unlikely to please all stakeholders. Nevertheless, officiating issues have
plagued sports leagues (e.g., the Tim Donaghy scandal in the NBA) and as
such, it may be worthwhile for sports leagues to be more amenable to dissent from players and team personnel members. In other words, sports
leagues may want to provide outlets where dissent can be directly communicated to league personnel, and perhaps lessen the discipline and financial
penalties. In doing so, athletes and sports figures may be less likely to publicize their grievances yet may still feel empowered to voice their concerns
in a meaningful way.

Sports franchises experience both ends of the dissent spectrum. On the
one hand, they have frustrations with sports leagues yet also are on the
receiving end of dissent from athletes. Social media offers a conduit for athletes to express displeasure with organizational decisions, especially when
they are directly affected. For instance, on July 28, 2009, football striker
Darren Bent was removed from the Tottenham Hotspurs flight to China
for a preseason tour moments before the plane was to take off. Tottenham
had arranged to transfer Bent to the Sunderland franchise and Bent was
aggravated. He turned to Twitter to direct critical comments toward
Tottenham chairman Daniel Levy, "Do I wanna go Hull City. No. Do I
wanna go Stoke. No. Do I wanna go Sunderland. Yes. So stop -------
around Levy." Then, "Why can't anything be simple? It's so frustrating
hanging around doing jack ----. Seriously getting ------ off right now.

Sunderland are not the problem in the slightest" (Wilson, 2009, p. 9). On July 31, 2009, Bent issued an apology for his Twitter comments and was subsequently fined 120,000£ ($186,442 USD). Despite this financial penalty, Bent acknowledged that he would continue to use Twitter. He indicated that he would ensure future posts were more "lighthearted" and claimed that he had learned from "his mistakes" (Hickman, 2009, p. 90).

Similarly, on February 28, 2010, San Diego Chargers linebacker Shawne Merriman learned that the Chargers had placed a restrictive tender on him, an action that greatly hampered his impending free agency. This move exercised contractual options that required any team signing Merriman to compensate the Chargers with first- and third-round Draft choices (essentially ensuring that Merriman would not receive a lucrative contract offer from another club). Accordingly, there was minimal interest in Merriman on the free-agent market and he was naturally upset (Davis, 2010). Where did he take his frustration? To Twitter. His tweets included the following, "Speechless today," "business is business, but some things just aren't right," and "I might take my 'high' tender money and donate it this year what you think about that?" Additionally, on July 16, 2009, Cincinnati Bengals kicker Shayne Graham voiced his frustration when his team did not offer him a contract extension. The Bengals had placed the "franchise tag" (an option that pays the player the average of the top five salaries at their position, but significantly prohibits the ability to change teams) on Graham and requested that he take a "discount" to remain with the team. Graham turned to Facebook to express his frustration, "How can a team give you the franchise tag showing your value to them, but not agree to a long-term deal because they want a discount. Makes no sense. Uugggghh" (Kirkendall, 2009).

In addition to dissenting about contractual status, athletes are using social media to convey displeasure with their playing time. For example, in August 2009, Australian track athlete Tasmyn Lewis posted critical commentary on Facebook after she was not selected to compete in a 400-meter hurdles event. Lewis stated, "I did a time trial of 56.8 on my own, my second fastest time ever, yet apparently I am not in shape to run at worlds. If you are in charge, communication is important, so is organisation, however, if you pay peanuts you get monkeys" (Gullan, 2009, p. 59). Lewis was subsequently disciplined for this commentary. In September 2009, Jets receiver David Clowney tweeted that he was frustrated with his lack of playing time. Jet head coach Rex Ryan later informed reporters that he was benching Clowney for poor performance in practice, but also disclosed that Clowney's tweet had confirmed his decision (Cimini, 2009b).

Whereas Lewis and Clowney directly voiced their displeasure over playing time, social media also enables an athlete's associates to express critical commentary about the organization. These messages may be a guise for an athlete's genuine feelings, yet conveniently remove authorship from the athlete while still getting their views disseminated. On November 7, 2009, shortly after the Montreal Canadians lost to the Tampa Bay Lightning, Allan Walsh, the agent for Canadians goalie Jaroslav Halak, who was involved in a battle for playing time with teammate Carey Price, criticized Price on Twitter. His tweet declared, "Interesting stat of the night … Price is 10W, 32L in last 42 starts. Hmm." This message started a firestorm within the Canadians' organization and Walsh quickly deleted the message from his Twitter account (Stubbs, 2009). Similarly, in May 2009, the Jets were engaged in contact negotiations with Alvin Keels—the agent for running back Leon Washington. Apparently frustrated by the lack of progress in the talks, Keels began tweeting about the negotiations, framing the Jets unfavorably. Keels disclosed that the Jets were "talking sideways in negotiations," and then acknowledged that "the Jets are a little ticked at me right now" (Cimini, 2009a). After the 2009-2010 NFL season, Washington was traded to the Seattle Seahawks.

Frustration with playing time and disagreements over personnel decisions creates divergence between athletes and sports organization personnel. Athletes may be uncomfortable voicing these concerns directly to coaches and other executives, thus social media offers a less-threatening venue to share these feelings. Furthermore, given the interactivity fostered on these sites, using social media to voice these feelings also facilitates public discussions about their grievances. For example, during the 2010 NBA playoffs, Los Angeles Lakers player Ron Artest used Twitter to voice his apparent displeasure with head coach Phil Jackson. On Thursday, May 6, 2010, a barrage of tweets began appearing on Artest's Twitter account criticizing Jackson. The first tweet declared, "Finally Phil Jackson didn't mention me in media before talking me Now I can build on game 2. Hopefully he talks to me before the media." The next one stated, "Ever since phil mention things about me in media before come to me first I was weird. So ever pray he can somehow close his yapper." The next tweet expressed, "Its just something that I have to get use to. He is a different style coach. Just bad timing during playoffs and midseason for me!!" Then finally, "I think right now the team is improving so we just need to keep building or moving ahead or forward. Locking down etc." (McMenamin, 2010).

These disclosures attracted significant media attention. This situation then grew more interesting when Artest's brother Daniel reported via his Twitter account that Artest's account had been hacked, and thus, the offending tweets were being sent by an imposter. Artest was vague in answering questions about the incident, although when shown a transcript of the tweets, he stated "I'll handle it" (McMenamin, 2010). It will likely never be known whether Artest's tweets were authentic. However, it should be noted that Jackson was particularly tough on Artest during the 2010 playoffs, and in that respect, it would not be surprising if Artest was the author. A related incident occurred on September 20, 2009, during an NFL game between the Arizona Cardinals and Jacksonville Jaguars. Marcus Fitzgerald, the younger brother of star Cardinals wide receiver Larry Fitzgerald, began sending tweets from Larry Fitzgerald's Twitter account. These messages indicated that his brother was upset that he was not being sufficiently used to that point in the game (Bickley, 2009). Some of the tweets also included derogatory comments about Cardinals quarter-back Kurt Warner, prompting speculation that turmoil existed between Warner and Fitzgerald (Sharp, 2009).

Authenticity is an important social media issue for both athletes and sports organizations to consider. If an athlete's social media account is compromised, this may free the athlete from culpability for any offending messages. However, proving that the account was hacked may be difficult and could be a deniability mechanism to blur authorship. Even if messages do come from a disingenuous source, this rarely quells media attention, as the dissent leveled at the sports organization initially appears to be coming from the athlete, and athletes can easily deny responsibility for problematic messages. However, in cases where a close associate is determined to be authoring content, it is possible that athletes might be influencing the commentary or using the person as a ghostwriter. Athletes who give family members and friends access to their social media accounts causes further complications for sports organizations to manage social media. These people may be privy to confidential information that athletes have shared with them but do not hold any obligation to keep this information private (or they may feel less inclined to do so). Moreover, there is little recourse for sports organizations to prevent these people from publicizing information. Nevertheless, the potential for controversy remains. As such, it may be beneficial for sports organizations to discuss with athletes the issues that can manifest when they share access to their accounts. Such conversations may promote diligence and safeguarding of social media profiles, thereby mitigating potential social media issues.

Social media is a viable mechanism through which athletes and sports figures can express dissent. Social media publicizes dissent, generating media attention and discussion about these issues. Athletes and sports figures also gain control over the timing and content of their expressions of dissent, allowing them to support their claims with evidence and provide solutions, thereby increasing the perceived credibility of their issues (Kassing, 2005). Thus, dissent is bolstered and the public may be more likely to resonate with and support it, potentially pressuring sports organizations to be more receptive to these grievances. Sports organizations have little tolerance for dissent, as evidenced by the strong discipline enacted when it occurs, inherent risks involved in dissenting (Kassing, 2007). Social media offers a unique way for athletes and sports figures to integrate the public into their dissent, which may shift sports organizations to adopt more accepting views toward dissent.

Using social media to voice dissent may damage relationships between athletes and team personnel members. Expressing dissent via social media is a form of circumvention—a dissent strategy where one voices his or her disagreements to those outside the supervisory chain of command (Kassing, 2002, 2009a). Sports organizations may expect that athletes will dissent through proper upward communication channels. Thus, when athletes deviate from this prescribed system, it may violate relational norms (Afifi & Metts, 1998; Burgoon, 1993). However, traditional channels may have previously proven ineffective and organizational culture may dictate a "no bad news" approach. Thus, social media is a less-threatening, albeit more public way to voice these concerns.

Additionally, the organizational hierarchy might not always be conducive to dissent. Kassing (2002) observed that employees sometimes voice dissent by consistently bringing the matter to their supervisor's attention over time. This strategy carries with it the risk for frustrating supervisory personnel with repetitive grievances. If athletes and sports figures have attempted to address issues internally without satisfactory results, social media allows them to publicize their dissent to external audiences. To that end, sports organizations should be cautioned about categorizing social media dissent as "sour grapes." These expressions may be harbingers of larger organizational problems and if not addressed internally, could bring unwanted media and public attention to the organization. The case involving former Texas Tech head football coach Mike Leach exemplifies this outcome. Leach responded to criticisms voiced by players over Twitter by forbidding them to use Facebook and Twitter. This directive effectively shut down avenues for players to report problems with Leach's management of the program—the issue that that essentially led to his termination.

Organizational culture may dictate the extent to which athletes, coaches, and administrators are encouraged to discuss issues, and there are many players who do not dissent publicly. Nevertheless, with the capabilities social media offers, sports organizations may need to re-evaluate their approach to dissent. For example, rather than imposing universal discipline for all organizational critiques, crafting joint public responses that acknowledge frustration exists and offering potential solutions may prove more fruitful. Discipline and sanction certainly have their value; however, this may not always be the most strategic option. Indeed, dissent varies in magnitude, suggesting that sports organizations delineate between expressions that warrant administrative action and those that may be better handled using alternative methods.

In re-examining organizational views toward dissent, it would be beneficial for sports organizations to work collectively with athletes and other vested parties (e.g., players associations) to determine when public dissent "crosses the line." Such collaboration may reduce uncertainty about organizational expectations for social media use. Additionally, participative approaches may reduce the need for organizations to ban social media entirely. Consider this announcement from football club Manchester United, one of the world's most recognizable sports franchises:

> The club wishes to make it clear that no Manchester United players maintain personal profiles on social networking websites. Fans encountering any web pages purporting to be written by United players should treat them with extreme skepticism. Any official news relating to Manchester United or its players will be communicated via ManUtd.com, the club said in its statement. (MacMillan, 2010, p. 1)

Additionally, during the 2010 Winter Olympics in Vancouver, British Columbia, the IOC instituted very structured social media policies. Athletes were prohibited from using social media during competition, from displaying the Olympic rings in any posting, and from reporting competition results. Additional exclusions were posting photos or videos from competition and mentioning corporations who were not "official Olympic sponsors" in their posts. Thus, although athletes could discuss their personal experiences at the Olympics, they could not report on the games (van Hemert, 2010).

Furthermore, re-evaluating the time frames in current social media policies may be warranted. A fine issued to Milwaukee Bucks player Brandon Jennings indicates why such a step may be needed. On December 20, 2009, Jennings was fined $7,500 by the NBA for violating the league's social media policy—tweeting before the postgame time restrictions had elapsed. Jennings' tweet was as follows: "Back to 500. Yes!!! '500' means where doing good. Way to Play Hard Guys" (FoxSports.com, 2009). Jennings was clearly excited about his team's performance and was praising his teammates for their ability to endure.

Yet, he was fined because this message fell inside the time restrictions outlined in the NBA's social media policy. In this case, Jennings was showing enthusiasm and evidencing his pride in the team's performance. This message likely encouraged both his teammates and Bucks fans—highly positive outcomes. Thus, based on this content, it may have been more prudent to warn Jennings about violating the policy or ignoring the infraction, suggesting the need to look at each incident on a case-by-case basis. That is, if unconditional censure is doled out, regardless of content, it may foster negative correlations toward social media, prompting athletes and sports figures to stop using these tools. In response to the fine, Jennings framed his actions as a "rookie mistake" and stated "it was a lesson learned, and I'll move on from it" (FoxSports.com, 2009). This suggests that broadcasting enthusiasm and pride in a team's accomplishments is a "mistake" that one must "learn from." The NBA is likely not intending to send such a message, but such interpretations seem likely to result when discipline is carte blanche. Accordingly, policies that emphasize content rather than timing might be more productive.

It is certainly understandable that sports organizations want to limit public criticism and prevent information leaks. However, by banning social media completely, they may be closing off important avenues for players to connect with fans, interaction that could benefit the organization. For instance, organizations could initiate promotions through player's Twitter postings that would drive interest in the team and increase revenues. Many players have hundreds of thousands and even millions of followers, and these audiences seem to be underused by sports organizations. Thus, rather than closing off these avenues entirely, it may be prudent to develop ways that both the sports organization and athletes can benefit from collaborative social media campaigns.

Additionally, implementing restrictive social media polices may actually increase controversy and public relations issues. For instance, although the Chargers likely were upset with Antonio Cromartie using Twitter to complain about training camp food, the attending support he received from his colleagues fueled publicity. In this situation, speaking with Cromartie about the team's concern and not fining him may have been more conducive. These policies also do not guarantee that players will stop using social media and may prompt them to more assertively circumvent them. Thus, as these examples suggest, intense regulation is likely to exacerbate tensions about social media and it may be more beneficial for collaborative approaches to be used.

Although polices are important in guiding organizational behavior, sports organizations may need to re-evaluate their policies as social media continues to expand. Indeed, regularly evaluating social media policies will enable sports organizations to stay abreast of the technological capabilities these media offer. One way that these policies may be bolstered is through negotiation that establishes privacy rules and boundaries for social media use. Accordingly, the chapter concludes by exploring how such process could unfold using Communication Privacy Management (CPM) theory (Petronio, 1991) as a guiding framework.

Management of private information appears to be the central issue driving social media conflict in sport. This task is largely communicative (A. Miller, 2009) and CPM theory offers five suppositions (Petronio, 2002) that have significant utility for social media policies in sports organizations. The first supposition considers private disclosures to reveal aspects of the self that are not publicly known—information people perceive that they have the right to control. Athletes and sports personalities are using social media to share personal information at unprecedented levels. These disclosures give fans intimate glimpses into what these individuals are thinking and feeling about a variety of issues—including frustration at work. For fans, obtaining these insights and possessing the ability to respond to them via social media fosters perceptions of humanness that promote conversation (Kelleher, 2009; Kelleher & Miller, 2006). Additionally, these opportunities are difficult for fans to experience in face-to-face contexts, which drives them to social media sites to dialogue with athletes and sports figures. As these interactions occur, they promote intimacy and a willingness to elevate information disclosures.

Not surprisingly, sports organizations encourage athletes to use social media, but organizational expectations about message content are unclear. This ambiguity sends mixed messages to athletes and sports figures, who may perceive that any subject is "fair game." Thus, when they are disciplined for message content, it may incite conflict, as athletes and sports figures perceive that their commentary reflects their individual experiences, information they have the right to release. It seems beneficial then, for sports organizations and athletes to craft policies that clearly delineate between personal and shared information and the conditions under which joint information can be released.

This leads to CPM's second supposition, which involves determining whether information is private or public. People share or withhold information according to previously established criteria or negotiated rules. This suggests that sports organizations and athletes need to negotiate about what information may be publicly shared. For instance, these parties may agree that athletes can post commentary about their own feelings, but refrain from revealing information about another player. As sports organizations take more reflexive and cooperative perspectives toward social media, athletes and sports figures may feel less burdened by organizational mandates. Instead, they may perceive more autonomy in their social media use, thereby reducing conflict—an outcome for which CPM's third supposition accounts.

This tenet suggests that people feel both vulnerable and violated when they lose control over information dissemination. Additionally, these feelings also occur when privacy is invaded (through both external monitoring and confidants disclosing information they were instructed not to share), and as risks associated with various information-management processes are realized. This suggests the need for sports organizations to clearly dictate what information remains in the organization's control and what information players and other personnel may release. In doing so, boundaries are established that provide clear guidelines. Moreover, once these boundaries are agreed on, sports organizations may need to "live" with the results and refrain from discipline unless content is highly problematic (e.g., disclosing illegal activity or actions that have severe consequences, such as "importing" groupies). This understanding also seems likely to facilitate more amicable relations between sports organizations and athletes in managing social media. For instance, athletes may feel more support and less intrusion from sports organizations and reciprocate accordingly. Thus, rather than broadcasting confidential information via social media networks, they may withhold this information as well as critical commentary.

Furthermore, in determining appropriate social media boundaries, it would be prudent for sports organizations to caution athletes and other personnel about giving others access to their social media profiles. CPM's fourth supposition states that when people share information, others become co-owners of that knowledge, which requires the development of privacy rules. These rules typically govern: (a) who receives the disclosure; (b) when, how much, and where disclosures occur; and (c) ways that a person might conceal this information (Petronio, 2002). Transferring these rules to social media polices may assist sports organizations in reducing the potential for sensitive information being publicly released. For example, sports organizations may withhold pending personnel changes from athletes until they are ready for a public response. Similarly, sports organizations may release information in fragments, to give them more time to prepare for the news being publicly shared.

However, creating rules alone is insufficient, these guidelines and boundary conditions must then be managed. Petronio (2002) identified three privacy rule management processes: (a) privacy rule development and attributes; (b) rules that moderate boundary linkages, boundary ownership rights, and boundary permeability; and (c) issues related to boundary turbulence. It would be advisable for sports organizations to incorporate these features as they manage social media. It seems pertinent for creation of privacy rules to be a collaborative process. On both sides, these negotiations should reflect a willingness to compromise. Additionally, as rules are developed, it would be advisable to determine what types of information each group owns and when information release violates boundary expectations. For example, athletes may be free to voice dissent via their social media account, but if this dissent becomes divisive or harmful, it oversteps the boundary.

An important facet of such discussions is the recognition that social media dilemmas will still occur. Accordingly, it is necessary to agree on appropriate action steps when these situations take place. For instance, when missteps happen, a public response may be collectively crafted, which may include clear steps to prevent similar missteps. To that end, social media training is a tool that can be used to mitigate issues. Although athletes do receive media training, social media is an entirely distinct domain from face-to-face interaction. With social media, athletes have significant control over message content and there is little filtering to prevent troublesome disclosures. Indeed, some sports organizations are advising athletes to treat social media messages as though they were speaking in front of a camera (Zelkovich, 2009). Furthermore, social media training can incorporate research that integrates athletes' motivations for using social media. This data may greatly assist sports organizations as they enact preventative measures. For example, athletes who use social media to criticize the organization because they feel that their previous requests have been ignored would alert sports organizations to a problem. Thus, sports organizations could then rework existing internal mechanisms to promote more effective responses to grievances that may prevent them from appearing on social media networks.

Moreover, sports organizations may need to offer resources and supports to athletes who become addicted to social media. Although it may be difficult to believe that a person could become addicted to social media, research has found that people can become addicted to technological devices (Perry & Lee, 2007). The case of NFL player Shawn Andrews offers a compelling example of this condition. On March 17, 2010, the Philadelphia Eagles released Andrews from the team. Andrews had missed the previous season due to injury, but *Philadelphia Inquirer* reporter Jeff McLane suggested that Andrews' Twitter use contributed to his release (McLane, 2010). Another *Inquirer* article chronicled some of Andrews' tweets, recounting that in one 24-hour period, he tweeted 134 times, or roughly every 10 minutes (Gonzalez, 2010). This article argued that Twitter had become an "addiction" for Andrews as evidenced by his diverse tweets ranging from his excessive food consumption to commentary about his neighbors sexual activity. Whether this factored into the team's decision to release Andrews is only speculative, but Andrews' behavior mimics signs displayed by people suffering from Internet addiction (Kim & Haridakis, 2009; LaRose, Lin, & Eastin, 2003). Sports organizations may need to be proactive in helping players if they began displaying excessive social media tendencies. Providing these resources also promotes goodwill that elicits more conducive social media relations.

In adopting participative approaches to social media management, it is important to plan for challenges. The goals, attitudes, and preferences for social media vary, so it may be difficult to establish satisfactory policies. CPM's fifth supposition is that competing goals and interests emerge as people determine desirable privacy and publicity levels. Such tension manifested in commentary from NBA player Matt Barnes after he was told to modify his social media use. Barnes stated that he had been told by "higher powers" to "tone down his language" on his tweets. Barnes discussed the dialectical tensions inherent in social media, acknowledging that although players publicly represented the league, he believed that the monitoring was "over the top" (J. Miller, 2010).

Barnes further argued that players should be able to disclose "their true feelings" and contended that fans wanted "to know how we're feeling . . . they don't want us to sugarcoat it. . . . It's really one of the only ways for fans to know what we're doing, our true feelings" (J. Miller, 2010). Interestingly, Barnes responded to this directive by presenting the issue to his Twitter followers, "Wit that said I was bothered when they told me that, cause I thought u were suppose 2 b urself on twitter, Wata yall think?" (J. Miller, 2010). Sports organizations and athletes must account for their competing social media goals and diligently look for ways to complement these desires. For instance, if sports organizations want athletes to use social media as a vehicle to connect with fans, they may need to tolerate some content or adopt reflexivity with the timing of social media messages.

In summary, social media has introduced a multitude of challenges for sports organizations. Sports organizations have less control over information being released to the public and it would be impossible to regulate every potential way this could occur. Approaching this issue with highly regulative and restrictive policies seems to have little effect on stemming problematic disclosures. Additionally, the tighter the organizational grip on social media, the more assertively athletes look to circumvent these policies. Consider this tweet from San Diego Chargers player Shawne Merriman during training camp in 2009, "Coach said we cant tweet in the blding so i called my lawyer and found a lupo in that contract ... tweeting outside yeaaaaa" (Maese, 2009).

Social media is here to stay. Although athletes may eventually move away from Twitter and Facebook to the next hot social media channel, the implications and challenges these media create will only intensify. These mediated platforms offer athletes a wealth of communicative advantages and fans are heavily following athletes' social media activity. Working together, sports organizations, athletes, and other stakeholders can transform social media into a strategic partnership rather than a reliable conflict source.

4

CLOSER TO THE ACTION
CONNECTING ATHLETES AND FANS

One of the more dynamic outcomes produced by social media is the increased ability for fans to access athletes. Social media acts as a conduit that connects these two groups, serving as a communicative bridge that facilitates interaction opportunities. Fans can certainly interact with athletes on a face-to-face basis; however, these encounters are limited, and rarely offer fans sufficient time to engage in meaningful conversation. Social media enhances perceptions that athletes and sports figures are "closer" to fans as they gain digital and physical access. This capability was vividly evidenced by Arizona Cardinals player Darnell Dockett. On July 21, 2010, Dockett tweeted, "Call me let's chat, but I don't wanna talk about football [lists phone number]." Dockett did take several calls, which fans confirmed on his Twitter profile:

> "Just talked 2 'Nine-O' ... didn't think he'd really answer, real cool dude!"
>
> "Just got off the phone with @ddockett lol real cool dude—thanks Bro"
>
> "Just got off the phone with @ddockett. Legit how dude talks to fans via the phone."

"I just talked 2 @ddockett he is a great guy he promised me he will not cut his hair God bless him oh he has a very sexy voice!"

Although Dockett certainly could not answer every call, the voice mail answering associated with the number stated that the caller had reached his "fan line" and that he would make an effort to return the call. Social media was an optimal venue for Dockett to release this information and those following him on Twitter gained a very unique way to interact with him.

This is but one example of the interactive possibilities taking place between fans and athletes across social media. Social media presents fans with unprecedented access to athletes and some athletes have hundreds of thousands or millions following their social media activity. Indeed, Jim DeLorenzo, vice president of the sports marketing agency Octagon Digital, noted that tweets from athletes are "often compelling by nature *simply because of their source*" (Lemke, 2009, p. A1, italics added). In following athletes and sports figures via social media, fans gain intimate perspectives that would be unlikely to appear in the mainstream media and they can respond directly to these individuals. Additionally, fans can access athletes and sports figures when it is convenient and are able to construct meaningful messages. Such capabilities enhance perceptions of intimacy and closeness, regardless of whether fans ever receive an actual response. In fact, research suggests (Kassing & Sanderson, 2009, 2010; Sanderson, 2008b, 2008c) that social media greatly facilitates parasocial interaction. These displays mirror behavior that a person would enact towards someone with whom they had an actual social relationship, but differs because it is one sided and unreciprocated (Horton & Wohl, 1956).

Through social media messages, fans can enact a wide range of behaviors toward athletes and sports figures. For instance, fans provide intricate advice to help athletes overcome performance struggles and express support and encouragement to athletes as they confront both personal and athletic issues. Conversely, fans also criticize athletes for subpar performance, degrade them for personal misconduct and chastise them for leaving sports teams. Social media also fosters connections between fans and amateur athletes. Social media also gives fans unprecedented access to amateur athletes. Fans can follow these athletes through their high school competition, which promotes attachment. These feelings intensify as these athletes complete high school and face decisions about continuing their athletic career at the collegiate level. Collegiate-level athletic recruiting (primarily football and basketball) is one of the most visible sporting practices to be affected by the Internet. There are multiple sites that offer fans recruiting information on a year-round basis and that eagerly invite fan participation and commentary. Coverage on these sites is so extensive that fans can follow the careers of athletes who are several years away from even being eligible to make college decisions, yet players are receiving notoriety at younger ages. This trend was vividly magnified during the 2010 college football recruiting season when USC received a verbal commitment from David Sills, a quarterback from Bear, Delaware—*Sills is a 13-year-old junior high student* (Pompey, 2010; Weiss, 2010).

In addition to facilitating communication between fans and athletes, social media also enables fans to advocate on behalf of athletes and sports figures. These actions may be inconsequential to sports organizations; nevertheless, they are becoming increasingly popular ways to both display fandom and enact social support. The case of former Texas Tech University head football coach Mike Leach provides a compelling example where these social media functions came into play. On December 30, 2009, Texas Tech University fired Leach amid allegations that he had mistreated player Adam James—the son of former NFL player and current ESPN college football analyst Craig James. James alleged that on December 17, 2009, one day after he had sustained a concussion, he was directed by medical personnel to not practice. After relaying these instructions to Leach, James claimed that Leach notified a team trainer to put him in "the darkest place, to clean out the equipment and to make sure that he could not sit or lean" (Schad, 2009). Leach adamantly proclaimed his innocence and when Texas Tech announced his dismissal, fans promptly took up sides to defend both Leach and James in a most unlikely battleground—Facebook. Fans created multiple Facebook groups including, "Keep Mike Leach," "Save Mike Leach," and "Adam James rules." Others supported Leach by denigrating James. For instance, "I hate Adam James," "Adam James = Douche Bag," and "Adam James is a bitch! BRING LEACH BACK!"

Similarly, on June 2, 2010, MLB umpire Jim Joyce erred in calling a Cleveland Indians runner safe at first base, costing Detroit Tigers pitcher Armando Galarraga a perfect game (a game in which a pitcher does not allow any opposing batters to reach base). Had Joyce made the correct call, the game would have ended with Galarraga's historic feat being recorded in baseball history. Galarraga subsequently retired the next batter and the Tigers won the game. After the game, Joyce was shown his erroneous call and became extremely remorseful. Both Galarraga and the Tigers franchise graciously accepted Joyce's apology, and recognized the incident for what it was—an employee who made a "real-time" mistake under intense pressure. However, fans were not so forgiving and turned to Facebook to voice their contempt toward Joyce. Facebook groups began emerging that included, "Fire Jim Joyce," "Jim Joyce Blew It," and "F*ck you Jim Joyce." Even Michigan Governor Jennifer Granholm joined in the social media protests by tweeting that she was recognizing Galarraga's perfect game. She then issued an official proclamation declaring that Galarraga pitched a perfect game (Riley, 2010).

Social media is a viable mechanism for people to display their fandom, a significant social identity component (Hirt, Zilmann, Erickson, & Kennedy, 1992). Sports organizations are using social media to increasingly involve fans in events, thereby elevating fandom. For instance, during the 2010 MLB first-year player Draft, the league incorporated tweets from audience members into their Draft coverage. Specifically, MLB used a Twitter feed with two options—"Everyone" and "Insiders." To be included in the "Everyone" feed, one only needed to include the "#mlbdraft" hashtag (using the # sign or "hashtag" allows one to easily search Twitter for subject material, in this case, tweets about the MLB draft) in their tweets. Entrance to the "insiders" forum, however, required fans to diligently watch for and respond to special access offers (Newman, 2010). Additionally, NFL commissioner Roger Goodell has tweeted commentary during the NFL Draft and some NFL teams are revealing Draft picks on Twitter before they are announced officially (Newman, 2010; Zillgitt, 2009). Those fans who follow league personnel and sports organizations on Twitter gain "insider" access (Kassing & Sanderson, 2010) to information that they can then relay via their individual social media accounts. Such interactivity may prompt fans to believe that they are "included" in decision-making processes, increasing perceptions that sports organizations need their input. These attributions then bolster their fandom and may allow them to derive social capital with other fans (e.g., a fan whose tweet is responded to by an athlete or league official).

As these brief examples indicate, social media increases connection and interaction between athletes and fans. Fans have unprecedented access to athletes, which facilitates both positive and negative communication. These capabilities have transformed social media forums into prominent sites where fans can display PSI toward athletes and sports figures.

PARASOCIAL INTERACTION

PSI describes how media users relate to and develop relationships with media figures (Horton & Wohl, 1956). Research suggests that PSI mirrors actual social relationships and that media users evaluate media figures in the same way they evaluate actual social partners (Giles, 2002). For instance, R. Rubin and McHugh (1987) found that social attraction to a media figure was a stronger predictor of PSI than physical attraction, and J. Cohen (2004) and Tsao (1996) argued that parasocial and actual social relationships required equivalent skill sets. Early PSI research focused on traditional mass media channels as scholars explored PSI with television newscasters (Palmgreen, Wenner, & Rayburn, 1980; A. Rubin, Perse, & Powell, 1985; R. Rubin & McHugh, 1987); soap opera characters (Perse & Rubin, 1989;

A. Rubin & Perse, 1987); and radio and television talk show hosts (A. Rubin, 2000; A. Rubin, Haridakis, & Eyal, 2003). Although traditional media has laid the foundation for PSI research, with the advent of social media, audience members have convenient tools that allow them to be more overt in expressing PSI. These actions are further bolstered as celebrities increasingly use social media channels to regularly solicit fan participation.

As PSI becomes more overt, more diverse behaviors manifest. Gleich (1997) identified a behavioral dimension of PSI—emphatic interaction. This concept refers to the behavioral or affective responses from viewers and is characterized by displays such as verbally addressing the media figure and feeling embarrassed when they make a mistake. Additionally, other research suggests that PSI includes feeling sorry for media figures when they make mistakes, missing them when they are gone, looking forward to seeing them, seeking information about them, and advising and counseling them (J. Cohen, 2004; A. Rubin et al., 1985; Sanderson, 2008c; Sood & Rogers, 2000). With the large number of athletes and sports figures now using social media, fans have convenient mechanisms to directly express PSI to these individuals. Accordingly, researchers are beginning to position athletes' social media sites as viable forums where PSI can be enacted.

Kassing and Sanderson (2009) examined PSI on cyclist Landis' blog during three crucial stages of the 2006 Tour de France (TdF) that ultimately led to winning the TdF (which was later stripped due to positive tests for performance-enhancing drugs). They discovered that people expressed PSI to Landis in diverse ways. For instance, some individuals shared how they drew significant inspiration from Landis' athletic performance and reinforced his importance as a role model. One person noted, "I am going to show this stage to my step son and use it as a lesson to never give up," whereas another individual noted that Landis' experience was a reminder "never throw in the towel, no matter how bad things look." More passionate declarations included, "Floyd is made of the best stuff our species can offer" and "man if we could all learn to pull ourselves together and fight like that" (p. 189).

Some people described the intense physical reactions they experienced as they watched Landis perform. One person noted that after watching Landis, they needed to "take the rest of the day off to recover." Others shared how Landis was disrupting their daily lives. One individual detailed how they were "reading live updates on my cell phone as I drove 70mph. . . . The whole time I was screaming alone in my car 'Come on Floyd!!!! Just keep going!!!!'" Another person stated:

> Floyd, it's a good thing my boss was out of the office this morning, because as I read the race updates, I couldn't help but shout from cubicle, "Open up that can of whupa$$, and ride Floyd, RIDE!" (p. 192)

Audience members also enacted relationally appropriate behaviors as they shared in Landis' success and disappointment. Thus, people conveyed empathy and encouragement when Landis experienced setbacks, then praised and congratulated him when was successful. Interestingly, after Landis recovered from his adversity, several fans acknowledged that they had doubted him and expressed remorse for their lack of faith. Examples included, "Please accept my apologies for thinking there was no way. I was not aware that there was ANYBODY in the world who could do what you did today," and "I told my wife today sadly that there was no way (sorry about that). But you said 'WAY!'" (p. 195).

Similarly, in Sanderson (2008c), I explored PSI on Curt Schilling's blog after two noteworthy incidents: (a) Schilling being accused of faking an injury; and (b) Schilling issuing an apology after publicly chastising fellow player Barry Bonds. Schilling had a fragile relationship with sports reporters, so it was not altogether surprising that he used his blog to distribute these messages—and fans promptly responded. I observed that PSI occurred by people (a) identifying with Schilling; (b) admonishing and advising him; and (c) criticizing him (this antisocial behavior is discussed later). Identification occurred by (a) establishing religious commonality; (b) sharing a common enemy—a mutual contempt for sports journalist Dan Shaughnessy; and (c) expressing admiration and respect for Schilling.

During his career, Schilling was quite open about his Christianity, which did bring criticism. Fans, however, were overwhelmingly supportive and appreciative of these pronouncements. Examples included, "I appreciate your comments about the Lord," and "I want to commend you on your willingness to speak up for your Lord and Creator" (p. 347). Furthermore, in response to Schilling disclosing that at times he had forgotten the Lord, one person reminded him:

> We've all had times in which we didn't glorify the Lord as much as we should have. Good thing he forgives and gives us 2nd, 3rd, 10 millionth chance. As for the press' reaction, the Lord knows this type of thing would happen. He offers this bit of comfort.

> Blessed are you when they revile and persecute you and say all kinds of evil against you falsely for My sake. 12 Rejoice and be exceedingly glad, for great is your reward in heaven, for so they persecuted the prophets who were before you. Matthew 5:11-12. (p. 346)

Fans also voiced their shared disdain for Shaughnessy by adopting Schilling's moniker for him "Curly Haired Boy—or CHB," in their postings. Others invoked more derogatory references describing Shaughnessy as a "maggot" and a "media slimeball" (p. 347). One person posted a letter written to Shaughnessy that included in part, "You are nothing more than a self righteous, self important, pontificating fool. You merely talk because you like to hear yourself. Why not do the rest of us a favor and shut up?" (p. 347). Fans also lauded Schilling for the way that he had managed personal adversity. In complimenting Schilling for his apology to Bonds, people declared, "To come out with an apology like this shows us the kind of guy you are," along with "Everyone is going to make mistakes, and its admirable that you held your hand up and dealt with it" (p. 348). For some, Schilling's commendable behavior cemented his status as a role model, "Most people don't have the guts/balls to fess up and admit that what they said was wrong. I can't tell you how much more of fan you made me and I didn't think that was possible," and "It takes a big man to admit he was wrong, especially on the public stage. Once again, you prove that you are a man of integrity" (p. 348).

PSI also extends to nonplaying personnel. Sports figures such as head coaches, general managers, and team owners are using social media to connect with fans. It is difficult to think of any sports owner or executive who maintains a stronger social media presence than Mark Cuban. Cuban regularly broadcasts information via Twitter and his blog. One of the more riveting ways that Cuban used social media occurred in 2007 as he promoted his appearance on ABC's popular television show *Dancing With the Stars*. Cuban consistently posted blog updates about his experiences on the show and encouraged fans to vote for him and his dance partner, disclosures that were well received by blog readers and that prompted PSI displays.

In Sanderson (2008b), I explored the PSI manifesting in these blog postings and discovered that PSI appeared as emphatic interaction (Gleich, 1997). Specifically, audience members (a) disclosed the emotional intensity they experienced as Cuban performed; (b) conveyed the diligent tasks that they were performing to preserve Cuban's tenure on the show; and (c) advised and counseled Cuban on ways to improve his dancing techniques to make him a stronger competitor. Similar to the emotional roller coaster that people experienced by watching Floyd Landis perform, audience members shared with Cuban the variety of emotions his dancing performance elicited. For instance, "I had such pleasure watching you dance tonight!!" and "My eyes got all welled up during your performance" (p. 160). After Cuban was nearly eliminated early in the competition, some people apologized for failing to vote for him. Expressions included, "I'm ashamed to admit that I didn't vote—I thought you were a shoe in," and "I apologize. It's all my fault. I had trouble getting my son to bed during the time allotted to vote, so I did not get to" (p. 160). Interestingly, several individuals disclosed that watching Cuban perform had prompted them to change their perceptions about him:

> I must say I hated you during the Mavs/Heat series 2 year ago, being a huge Heat fan, but I have completely changed my mind and see that you are very charming and trying so hard to do your best at dancing.

And:

> Mark—I was so wrong about who you were—only "knowing" you as the owner of the Mavericks (and NOT a fan). I thought you were spoiled and liked to cause static, again, only because I knew you through what I saw during your games. . . . Please accept my apologies for misjudging your character; you are a wonderful motivator, a damn hard worker, and you always make me smile when I see you dance. (p. 161)

These strong emotional investments prompted some people to take tangible action to ensure that Cuban remained on the show, devotion that they proudly shared with him. For example, "MC: I sent out an email to EVERYONE, A blast of 14k to vote for you," and "However after shooting the stills of you and Kym last week working on your routine, I'm telling everyone don't bet against you" (p. 161). Others shared their proselytizing efforts, "My girls are telling everyone at their schools my husband at his work and I am sending out e-mails to all my girlfriends. I know this is a small portion, but sometimes that all adds up!!!" "This week I created a bunch of fake e-mail addresses and gave you guys more than 100 votes!!! lol . . . I will try to think of even more next week" and:

> I think I found a loophole in the voting system . . . I have a VOIP phone line hooked up through [names Web site]. DWTS let me vote an unlimited amount using the line—probably because of the weird caller ID values it sends. So I have no idea how many votes I sent in, but it was probably at least 200:). (pp. 161-162)

Social media's participative features facilitate PSI expressions. Fans can conveniently communicate these feeling along with the physical responses to these emotions. These exploits could certainly be shared via traditional communication channels; however, social media encourages perceptions that athletes and sports figures have "received" the fan's message. Letters can be lost in the mail, and even when correspondence arrives at team headquarters, it is combined with hundreds or thousands of others, limiting one's ability to receive a response. Although social media does not guarantee that athletes or sports figures will read fan messages, accessing these forums is more convenient than opening up hundreds of letters.

Additionally, athletes and sports figures use social media to initiate communication with fans. For example, former NFL quarterback Kurt

Warner routinely invites his Twitter followers to ask him questions. On June 1, 2010, he tweeted, "Alright y'all … you guys are dragging a little, gonna have to catch up with you tomorrow" and then, "GOING ONCE, GOING TWICE" and then "GONE!!!" Then on June 2, 2010, "Any of you gonna bring anything unique and interesting tonight or am I going to be early. … It's in ur hands. … Kids going 2 bed soon!" Perusing Warner's Twitter account, it is evident that he responds to a variety of questions about diverse topics such as football, family, and religion. Similarly, on May 11, 2010, NBA player Chris Bosh tweeted, "Ok twitter. Let's have a conversation! Ask me questions and I'll answer, but nothing basketball related." Bosh then spent time answering questions about his tastes in music, cars, and movies he had watched.

On May 21, 2010, Phoenix Suns player Jared Dudley used Twitter to seek recommendations on how the Suns could beat the Los Angeles Lakers. At the time, the Lakers were ahead 2–0 (games) in the NBA Western Conference finals. Specifically, Dudley asked, "If there are 2 things we need to do better to win game 3 what are they? Be specific … What do y'all see out there?" Dudley indicated that he had more than 600 responses ranging from humorous commentary to pleas for the Suns play better defense and more consistently make their shots (B. Young, 2010). Additionally, on June 7, 2010, Phoenix Suns player Amare Stoudemire asked fans on Twitter to comment on his pending free agency. He asked, "I think about Free Agency Everyday. Should I Stay in Phoenix or should I leave? This the question of the Summer. What do you guys think?" On April 30, 2010, Bosh addressed his pending free agency by asking his Twitter followers, "Been wanting to ask. Where should I go next season and why?" He quickly clarified by asking, "OK … Let me rephrase the question. Should I stay or should I go?"

The likelihood that athletes and sports figures will read and perhaps respond to social media transmissions has prompted fans to increasingly offer advice and counsel in their messages. In some of the studies mentioned earlier (Kassing & Sanderson, 2009; Sanderson, 2008b, 2008c) advice-giving was a prominent finding. With Landis (Kassing & Sanderson, 2009), fans dispensed diverse counsel related to both cycling and social activities. For example, "Get some rest tomorrow and get those legs ready for Saturday!" "Tell those mechanics to CHECK and DOUBLE CHECK YOUR DAMN BIKE!!!" and:

> Therefore, after reflection, not only do I think you should attack, but you should attack from the beginning of the stage. Look, I'm not a professional cyclist by any means, but if you go out and the leaders think you're mad, you may just get away with something no one ever expected. (p. 196)

In Cuban's case (Sanderson, 2008b), fans shared advice designed to keep Cuban on *Dancing With the Stars*. Some people offered brief suggestions, "Just remember that dancing is an expression of yourself—relax and go with the flow," and "do *not* sing along! i know it's hard esp.—if you have a good song . . . but it's distracting and doesn't come across well on TV." Others expressed pointed, tactical counsel, "But you really need to work on being precise in your movements. . . . The crispness is still lacking from your performance," and:

> On the dances, please listen to Carrie-Ann [judge]. I think she has hit on a couple of points which would help increase your score. Firstly, you should keep your tongue in your mouth. It is dancing not basketball. You remind me of a Michael Jordan on the dance floor with his signature look of his tongue hanging out of his mouth. Secondly, you should not lip synch the songs you are dancing to. To be also to get to the top, you have to dance not lip synch, forget about Milli-Vanilli while you are dancing. Thirdly, just practice, practice, practice, as you are already doing, You will go far in this competition. But, you will need to make some these changes. (p. 162)

Fans' advice to Schilling (Sanderson, 2008c) was stern, bordering on reprimand. Some people told Schilling to focus more attention on baseball rather than blogging. For example, "Just play baseball and leave the judging part to God," "Fans pay your salary to see you pitch, not act like a tool. Just pitch bro," and:

> Sorry Curt, but you need to do a little less playing into the drama and get yourself into shape . . . mentally, physically, and emotionally. You could have done yourself a favor and burned a little less emotional energy on this and spent a little more time on the tread mill and in the gym. You came into camp completely overweight and out of shape. Then you demanded that the Sox give you an extension, when clearly you didn't look like you wanted or earned it. You look like hell, Curt. You shouldn't have time for this kind of drama. (pp. 348-349)

Some individuals advised Schilling to be more consistent in practicing his Christianity:

> Gary Thorne was on air admitting that he reported an inaccuracy and stated that it was a misunderstanding and that he was wrong. So again, I don't write this as a "come down" on you or as a session of "pointing the finger" but we've got to be examples of Jesus' love and patience as much as possible. (p. 349)

Another:

> But my reply to you here is your witness to the wider world is not
> godly. I remember the interview with you after the bloody sock game.
> You gave God all the glory at that time. Doesn't he deserve all the
> glory now? Where is he in all your blogging? God is not just a very
> present help in time of need. He is your life and breath and everything.
> Don't make it all about Curt. And as for using the Holy Scriptures like
> bullets, out of context, and out control, that is a danger also. (p. 349)

Although PSI displays often reflect relationally appropriate behaviors,
social media has facilitated an increasingly number of maladaptive PSI
enactments. Sanderson (2008c) found that people displayed negative PSI
toward Schilling by condemning him for his candor, overt religious displays, and his Republican Party affiliation and support for President
George W. Bush. Some audience members informed Schilling that his public commentary (including his blogging) reflected "what's wrong with our
country," and suggested that Schilling was "nothing but a media whore,
have been forever and will continue to be one." One person also declared:

> Curt you are a donkey!!! You love this publicity. The fact that you
> have a blog, call radio stations, and put your face in front of a camera
> every second possible shows how much of an attention seeker you are.
> . . . The announcer is an idiot, but then again so are you! (p. 350)

Still others derided Schilling for his overt religious displays, "The Lord
didn't help you pitch in a baseball game. The doctor and your talent did.
Take credit for your accomplishment. I doubt Jesus is a baseball fan," "By
the way, my Lord doesn't concern himself with how well you are pitching.
Even against the Yankees. He has violence against man and the earth to
worry about." Another person more elaborately stated:

> Reporters roll their eyes at your faith? Maybe because you are hypo-
> critical in your bashing of others and your judging and bitching. You
> also shove it down people's throats, just as you do your politics. Not
> everyone feels the need to wear their religion on their sleeve. When the
> Red Sox won the World Series in 2004, (yes thanks to your heroics
> which you deserve a permanent place in every Red Sox fan's heart for,
> and that of many others on the team too), you couldn't wait to pollute
> my voicemail with your political hucksterism. PLEASE spare me the
> whining!!!! Just try to ask yourself when you are tempted to bash oth-
> ers or blow off your mouth and offend others who don't necessarily all
> think like you do: What would Jesus do? I believe in Him too, and I

> seriously doubt he would act like you. You are so self righteous and
> holier than thou. (p. 351)

Some people were offended by Schilling's political views and expressed
their contempt through commentary such as, "Hey Curt, if you care so
much about 'integrity,' then why in God's name are you a Republican?"
"You were eager to endorse Bush back in 2004, so how about you share
with us your Iraq strategy?" One person suggested that Schilling's support
for Bush made him implicitly accountable for the consequences of the Iraq
War:

> You've got the blood of 3,373 (and counting) decent, dead American
> soldiers on your hands through your shilling for George Bush and
> Dick Cheney and their useless war. These deaths, and those of tens of
> thousands of other innocents in this war are what you should be talk-
> ing about, not some silly news report about a bloody sock. Shame on
> you. Have some integrity and Christian decency admit you made a
> mistake. Gary Thorne sure did. Apologize to the families who suffer
> their loss quietly. Jesus will forgive you. (p. 351)

Through social media, fans share in the exhilaration of athletes' and sports
figures' accomplishments and also counsel and condemn them when they
engage in behavior that violates fans' expectations. These behaviors are
heightened as athletes and sports figure capitalize on social media's interactive features to invite and encourage fan participation. As athletes and
sports figures increasingly solicit fans to offer input, these gestures foster
and enhance perceptions of closeness and intimacy. These feeling then trigger a diversity of PSI expressions.

Additionally, fans rarely have the opportunity to respond to requests
from athletes and sports figures in face-to-face contexts. These invitations,
enhanced by social media, have produced meaningful changes in athlete–fan
communication. Social media has given fans unprecedented access to athletes and sports figures. These connections foster feelings of intimacy, creating perceptions that fans have a "connection," and in some cases, a relationship with athletes and sports figures. As athletes and sports figures continue to solicit input from fans via social media, fans may perceive that
these individuals *need* their advice. Thus, fans may grow more direct in
their counsel, increasing the potential for conflict and hostility. Social
media requires no prerequisites for advice giving. Fans have no obligation
to offer any credentials that legitimates their input. Indeed, it seems that
fandom and media viewing is sufficient to qualify fans to dispense advice
from which athletes and sports figures can benefit.

Social media is increasing the propensity for fans enacting maladaptive behaviors towards athletes and sports figures. Research suggests that computer-mediated communication (CMC; of which social media is a component) can be more desirable than face-to-face exchanges (Walther, 1996). Communication scholar Joseph Walther labeled this concept the hyperpersonal model of computer-mediated communication (Walther, 1996). These perceptions result as CMC participants can selectively manage their self-presentation (Walther, 1992; Walther & Burgoon, 1992). This capability optimizes relational possibilities as self-presentation is not inhibited by social cues. Scholars have used the hyperpersonal model to demonstrate a number of positive outcomes (Peter & Valkenburg, 2006; Tidwell & Walther, 2002; Walther, Slovacek, & Tidwell, 2001). For example, this model has been applied to self-disclosures on Internet dating sites (Gibbs, Ellison, & Heino, 2006); to account for the willingness to "open up" and disclose information in online support groups (Walther & Boyd, 2002; Wang, Walther, Pingree, & Hawkins, 2008); and to predict trust in online relationships (Anderson & Emmers-Sommer, 2006).

Although these CMC features are certainly advantageous, they also can be used to demonstrate hyper "negative" behavior. The hyperpersonal model suggests that people's behavior is exaggerated when using CMC (Pena, Walther, & Hancock, 2007). Thus, CMC facilitates people to behave in ways that they would be unable to or unlikely to in face-to-face contexts. As such, social media sites, particularly those devoted to athletes, sports figures, and sports organizations, are prime venues for hyper "negative" behavior to occur. Moreover, as antisocial behavior at sporting events is well documented (Mean & Kassing, 2008; Palmer & Thompson, 2007; Wakefield & Wann, 2006) it seems likely that this behavior also would appear in social media domains.

In participating and interacting with athletes and sports figures via social media sites, fans become better acquainted with them. This is influenced by athletes and sports figures using social media to reveal personal information. These disclosures offer fans intimate access, insider information that rarely manifests via mainstream mass media channels (Kassing & Sanderson, 2010). This trend has generated several compelling outcomes, one of which is increasing identification for fans with athletes and sports figures.

IDENTIFICATION

Research suggests that individuals identify with celebrities when they perceive that they share similarities (Fraser & Brown, 2002; Jin, 2006; Soukup, 2006). For sports fans, these perceptions extend beyond athletes to include sports franchises and collegiate athletic teams (Wann, 2006; Wann & Branscombe, 1993) and constitute a significant component of their social identity (Hirt et al., 1992; Wann, Royalty, & Roberts, 2000). Social identity theory (Tajfel & Turner, 1986) contends that individuals have both a personal and a social identity. The theory also suggests that social identity is comprised of characteristics derived from demographic classifications or organizational memberships (Turner, 1982) and that people satisfy their self-esteem needs through group memberships (Tajfel & Turner, 1986). Once group membership is procured, people bolster self-esteem by forming favorable attitudes about their groups while positioning other groups as less valuable (Hogg & Abrams, 1999).These elements of social identity theory help explain how people become highly identified with athletes, sports personalities, or sports teams.

Indeed, sports fans often are highly invested in the performances of athletes and teams. For example, Gantz, Wang, Paul, and Potter (2006) found that sports fans were more emotionally involved and more likely to extend viewing experiences than were fans of other programming. Similarly, Fisher (1998) discovered that perceived similarity with sports teams was greatly influenced identification. Identification also extends beyond athletes and teams to include sporting venues. Trujillo and Krizek (1994) profiled fan reactions to the closing of two MLB stadiums—The Chicago White Sox's Old Comiskey Park and the Texas Rangers' Arlington Stadium. They discovered that fans possessed strong identification with these ballparks and commonly referred to the closing of "their" stadiums. Through these and similar disclosures, fans likened the ballpark closing to losing a close friend or family member.

Although fans bonded with these two ballparks, the prevailing trend of naming rights for sports stadiums may hinder these attachments. Boyd (2000) contended that as sporting venues become increasingly commodified, it reduces identity links. Specifically, many venues go through consistent naming changes, making it difficult for these locations to remain in the public consciousness. Although places such as Fenway Park and Wrigley Field still connect generations of sports fans, it is more difficult for memories to endure with stadiums whose naming corresponds with corporate mergers and acquisitions. Thus, most people could likely identify that Fenway Park is the home of the Boston Red Sox, but it may be more difficult to recall that Energy Solutions Arena is the home of the Utah Jazz.

Identification is visibly displayed at sporting events—fans painting their faces, wearing team or athletic apparel, and ridiculing opposing teams, players, and fans. Some sports teams have such immense identification with their fan base that they are culturally recognizable. For instance, the Cleveland Browns "Dawg Pound," the "Red Sox Nation," and Texas A&M University's "12th Man." Interestingly, the "12th Man" designation also is used by the NFL's Seattle Seahawks, which prompted legal action from Texas A&M. The lawsuit was eventually settled with both the Seahawks and Texas A&M being allowed to use this designation. However, the Seahawks acknowledged that Texas A&M possessed ownership rights to the term (Associated Press, 2006). Identification is a vital resource for sports organization to tap into, as highly identified fans are more likely to attend games and purchase team merchandise (Madrigal, 1995; Wakefield, 1995). Social media enhances the ability for identification to be fostered and displayed, thus it is not surprising that sports organizations have started official Facebook and Twitter profiles.

As identification intensifies, fans begin correlating their social identity with the performance of athletes and sports teams. Accordingly, fans invoke collective language such as "we" when describing these teams and athletes (Cialdini et al., 1976). For instance, consider this rebuke from a person who posted on Schilling's blog:

> in any situation where you represent my baseball team (and yes a sports talk radio show about baseball issues qualifies), I would greatly appreciate it if you would please stop the jousting and running battle with the media, avoid loaded questions, and keep your non-baseball opinions to yourself during the baseball season. You're a veteran, not a rookie. (Sanderson, 2008c, p. 349)

On a more troubling level, fan identification also may produce maladaptive behavior. Research has discovered that some fans are willing to engage in physical aggression toward opposing teams and players to give their team a competitive advantage (Wann et al., 2005).

Additionally, when athletes or teams are performing successfully, fans are more overt in expressing their "identification," whereas losing prompts fans to distance themselves (Partridge, Wann, & Elison, 2010). Yet, not all fans turn away from losing players or franchises. In fact, they may believe that these athletes or teams are cursed and unable to succeed because of some unseen force. For instance, many Boston Red Sox fans believed that the "Curse of the Bambino" (a perceived consequence from trading legendary baseball player Babe Ruth to the New York Yankees in 1918) prevented the team from winning a World Series for 86 years (Wann & Zaichkowsky, 2009).

Identification stems from perceptions of similarity. As athletes increasingly use social media to reveal personal information, these domains are prime venues for identification to develop. In disseminating personal topics, athletes share information that helps fans find points of connection. Consider these tweets from former Arizona Cardinals quarterback Kurt Warner, posted from May 31 to June 6, 2010:

"I can't even win at fam wiffle ball ... all down hill from here!"

"Morn all ... Payback stinks, just found out the house we were staying at got TPed last night. ... Great part i am gone and don't have 2clean up"

"Who lives w/o door on bathroom—a really close fam! It's kind of like motel 6, but not we'll 'leave light on',but 'put door on' for ya!"

"OK, 6yr old says he needs a BUCKET he is going to puke. So I get him bucket and he pukes, half way thru he stops and yells 'Told you DAD!'"

"6yr old starts feeling bad after visit to DairyQueen ... then pukes ... immediately following he announces 'He hates ICream, Never eating agin"

"Isn't it funny how growing up I couldn't stand look or smell of vomit ... now that I have kids I step in, catch, clean up without blinking"

"Up playing chess (or as my 6yr old calls it 'CHEST') w my son ... any tips, I really stink at it ...?"

Eating at fancy rest—my crew is spitting whole boiled eggs out of mouth, eating every type of food w hands and drinking w spoons! BigTip!"

"Ever been at a pool trying to relax, but there r screaming kids making it miserable?

Yeah, sorry, I apologize those r my kids!"

"2 4yr olds making a video in the BR with my phone w lights off. ... Any bets on how long til Dad needs a new phone or it smells like poop?"

"My wife told r kids she was an All-American cheerleader in HS. My son responded by saying what Nationality were other cheerleaders! Lol!"

Similarly, consider former New York Jets kicker Jay Feely, who was dubbed the team's "titan of Twitter" (G. Bishop, 2009, p. 1). Feely tweeted on a host of topics ranging from commentary on the H1N1 vaccine to his brother's struggle with muscular dystrophy. Feely's persistent tweeting hastened fans' ability to identify with him. Indeed, many fans felt that they "knew" Feely, a perception that was visibly demonstrated when one woman approached Feely and promptly listed the names of his children (G. Bishop, 2009).

Disclosures by Warner and Feely convey a "personal" side that brings fans intimate access into their personal lives, particularly as they relay stories that most fans have experienced in their lives. This is yet another way that social media facilitates closeness, particularly as athletes and sports figures share information that fans would be unlikely to obtain via the mass media. For example, had Warner disclosed the incident with his child getting sick in Dairy Queen to a reporter, it is unlikely it would have been included in an article or newscast. Yet, for a fan following Warner on Twitter, this story promotes commonality and bolsters identification toward Warner.

Cultivating identity through social media also enables athletes and sports figures to quickly solicit support. One of the more unique ways this occurred involved professional golfer John Daly. Daly asked his Twitter followers to harass sports journalist Gary Smits after Smits wrote an article disclosing disciplinary issues from Daly's PGA Tour file. Specifically, on March 2, 2010, Daly tweeted, "here's the JERK who writes NON-NEWS article on debut of my show—CALL & FLOOD his line and let's tell him how WE feel." The calls to Smits started around midnight—minutes after Daly sent the tweet (Gola, 2010, p. 73). Although most callers hung up, Smits reported that approximately 25% of callers left messages, some of which were quite abusive. Social media allowed Daly to quickly rally and obtain support from fans. Considering that his issue was with a reporter, had he voiced this information via the press, it is doubtful that fans would have obtained the necessary information (Smits' phone number) to act on Daly's behalf. Although it is unclear how many of the callers were following Daly on Twitter, it is noteworthy that calls begin pouring into Smits' office moments after Daly broadcasted this request.

Thus, social media offer athletes and sports figures access to large audiences composed of individuals who are ready and willing to support them—with or without invitation. These support mechanisms are available at little cost to the athlete, and provide quick return. Accordingly, social media sites become valuable public relations tools that allow athletes and sports figures to prompt fans to defend them.

SOCIAL MEDIA AND SUPPORT

The Internet has emerged as a popular mechanism for individuals to give and receive social support (Hlebec, Manfreda, & Vehovar, 2006). Research suggests that social support is often unsolicited (Goldsmith, 2004; Strauss & Falkin, 2001), and the interactive features of social media may influence these offerings becoming more prominent. Unsolicited support is likely to manifest on social media sites of athletes and other sports figures, allowing these individuals to obtain support without directly asking for it and enabling them to maintain face (e.g., avoid looking like a "whiner") and preserve identity (Sanderson, 2010). Moreover, considering that social media messages are visibly displayed, participants viewing supportive message may perceive that this behavior is the communicative norm.

Social support has a rich history in the sports world. For instance, during the 1952 World Series, Rev. Herbert Redmond of St. Francis Roman Catholic Church in Brooklyn, NY, implored his parishioners to pray for slumping Brooklyn Dodgers first baseman Gil Hodges (Clarridge, 2007). Additionally, in 2004, unexpected support was offered by traditionally ferocious and unsentimental Oakland Raiders fans to former Green Bay Packers quarterback Brett Favre during a game played shortly after his father's death (Cohn, 2004). Another example involved NBA superstar Earvin "Magic" Johnson. In 1991, after contracting HIV, Johnson retired from professional basketball. However, fans voted him to start in the NBA's 1992 All-Star game. Although the league restricted him from starting, an extra roster spot was created for Johnson and he did play in the game (Nance, 2007).

These examples highlight only some of the occasions in which fans have enacted social support toward athletes. Social media offers fans optimal communicative venues to express social support directly to athletes and sports figures. These individuals often receive significant media attention when they are experiencing troubling circumstances (e.g., missing a game-winning shot, being arrested). The ability to offer social support to athletes and sports personalities via social media is an important trend that is capturing research attention.

In Kassing and Sanderson (in press), we explored social support expressions by fans toward cyclist Landis as he battled allegations of using performance-enhancing drugs in capturing the 2006 TdF. We observed that people offered support to Landis in the following ways: (a) empathy and sympathy; (b) confirmation; (c) testimony; (d) sharing a common enemy; and (e) offerings. In voicing empathy and sympathy to Landis, fans discounted these allegations and acknowledged the strain Landis and his family were experiencing. For instance, the allegations were referred to as a "witch hunt," and a "nightmare," whereas another person added, "I am sure that this has been a tremendously challenging time in your life and the lives of your family members." Others disclosed that they were suffering with Landis, "I am so saddened that you have to go through this," and "I cried, I'm sorry for all the pain this must be causing!"

Through confirmation, fans bolstered Landis' identity and athletic accomplishments by affirming their trust in and loyalty to him. Examples included, "I just want to tell you that I've always believed in you and I will never doubt you are the true winner of the Tour de France. And that is that," along with "You are the one and only 2006 TdF champion regardless of what anyone says." Others proclaimed that Landis was an honest, hard-working athlete who "does not have time for bs and just wants to train and race hard," "the kind of man who would rather lose honestly than win dishonestly," "a man who can be taken at his word," "a rare pure class act," and "an American Hero!" This belief and trust toward Landis prompted others to proudly declare Landis' innocence, behavior that resembled religious witnessing.

These testimonials included, "Floyd, WE BELIEVE!" "We always believed in you, Floyd!" and "I believe in you. Stay the course." Others revealed their dedication and devotion in supporting Landis. People conveyed that they had supported Landis "from the beginning" and since "day one." Others boasted that, "I never questioned for 1 second you are innocent. No question, no suspicion, no doubt, not ever," "I've never doubted your innocence for a minute," and "I don't need any lengthy legal argument or scientific explanation. I've believed in you from the beginning." People also shared how their proselytizing efforts to convince skeptics of Landis' innocence. For example, "I keep telling all my friends that I believe you are not guilty and that you are not the type of person who would or needs to cheat," "I was cheering you on and have defended you to my friends and family," and "I will continue to believe in you, and get in anyone's face who says otherwise."

People rallied around Landis by voicing their contempt for his adversaries. These included the United States Anti-Doping Agency, the World Anti-Doping Agency, the International Cycling Union, and the French lab that conducted Landis' drug tests. Fans declared that these groups were "the most despicable untrustworthy people on the face of the earth," "blind AND stupid," and "worse than the old Communist Totalitarian Dictatorships." One person suggested that the manner in which these groups were treating Landis was "disgustingly evil." Thus, these organizations needed to be "brought out of the shadows and into responsibility before the world," "removed from further testing," and "closed down."

There were critics who infiltrated the blog and posted scathing commentary about Landis. This action prompted Landis' supporters to engage these detractors and defend him against their attacks. For example, critics were described as "beneath contempt," and "small people," who could not "even manage an intelligible sentence." Other castigations included, "At least learn how to spell loser before you throw the word around," and "I am guessing you would not even be able to buy a clue!! I am also guessing you don't have the words work ethic and determination in your vocabulary." One fan also provided a lengthy (584 words) defense that outlined itemized refutations of the criticisms being leveled at Landis. Through these actions, fans made it clear that floydlandis.com was an inappropriate venue for disparaging Landis, poignantly summarized by one person in this posting:

> A note for other bashers out there . . . if your IQ is less that the spoke count on Floyd's wheels you are at the wrong address and need to go over to iamaretard.com. . . . pretty much covers all of them I suspect.

Finally, fans encouraged Landis to notify them if there was any assistance they could provide to him. Some people offered this generally, "Don't be afraid to ask if there is something we fans can do," and "Let us know what we can do to help." Others offered specific assistance, particularly with helping Landis pay his legal fees. For example, "if you need money for the cause, let us know and I'll be the first to send what I can," and "Enough of cyclists believe in you and are so fed up with the situation that we might forgo a latte or two to help bankroll your efforts." Landis eventually started the Floyd Fairness Fund (FFF) as a mechanism for fans to contribute to his defense efforts and people promptly shared their donations to this cause. Examples included, "After much consideration for your situation & reworking my 2007 budget, I have decided to contribute to your fairness fund," "Since I couldn't get to the town meeting in Brooklyn I donated the fee anyway," and "Today, I have contributed to the FFF."

In Sanderson (2010), I examined social support on former Boston Red Sox pitcher Curt Schilling's blog. In this sphere, social support manifested as people validated Schilling's identity and framed him as an iconic figure in Red Sox history. The prominence of these postings transformed his blog into a space where fans mobilized to support and defend him. Schilling used his blog to criticize the mass media generally, and sports reporters specifically after a public allegation that he had faked an injury during the 2004 ALCS (ALCS). Fans overwhelmingly sanctioned these critiques and expressed their gratitude to Schilling for blogging. For instance, "It is a good thing you created this blog to speak directly with the fans of MLB, without having the media sully your message," and "it is so refreshing to hear things directly from an athlete instead of it being manipulated by the press" (p. 198). Others reinforced Schilling's blog as a tool that allowed him to retain control over media messages. Examples included, "This site is amazing because you are taking away ALL The power from the people who misuse their media credentials," and "keep blogging dude because it seems to really piss off lots of mediots that a star athlete has rendered their commentary less important" (p. 198).

People also disclosed empathy for Schilling, acknowledging that they would have reacted in a similar manner. These expressions included, "If I was in your position I would tell all the critics and so-called experts to go to hell (which you probably do anyways)," "I don't blame you for reacting like this. I'd be calling for the man's job if I'd been Swift Boated in the same way," and "Curt, as a person who also says what he thinks, often times to a fault, I can sympathize with you here." Additionally, after Schilling apologized on his blog for censuring Bonds during a radio interview, fans suggested that this commentary was attributable to the early time of the interview. For instance, "Hey I'm not a morning person either . . . it's hard to think straight just after you wake up," and "He's rethinking an 830AM interview. I would, too. I work second shift, too, and you wouldn't catch me dead, awake at 830AM" (pp. 198-199).

Although Schilling was criticized by sports reporters for these actions, fans emphatically reminded Schilling of his legacy within Red Sox culture. These feelings stemmed from Schilling's pivotal role in ending the Red Sox's 86-year World Series championship drought. Accordingly, criticism and negativity directed toward him was a temporary annoyance that had no effect on his collective significance to Red Sox fans. People shared, "All of us longtime fans in Red Sox Nation will be forever grateful to the gutsy effort displayed by Schilling during the incredible championship run," "we never would have brought home the championship without you!" and "the Red Sox won the 2004 world series and we could not have done it without curt schilling." Another person stated:

> Thanks for coming to Boston, thanks for being a tremendous and historic part of Red Sox baseball, thanks for not being so worried about what you marketing agents say to talk straight with the fans and community, thanks for not just paying lip service to history and fans of the Sox but actually immersing yourself, in both, thanks for the WORLD SERIES, and thanks in advance for just continuing to be yourself for as long as you're here. (p. 199)

Fans also displayed support for Schilling by suggesting that those who condemned him were not authentic Red Sox fans. These offerings were typified by commentary such as, "TRUE Red Sox fans support who you are, and what you do," "Your true fans know that you didn't fake the sock," and "I am with you, as well as the rest of the TRUE nation." Additionally, "All of us that are your fans know the truth," "All true baseball and red sox fans know that the blood was real," and "Any true Red Sox aficionado doesn't need proof—we already saw it." Some fans offered support through expressions of tangible action, "So from Red Sox Nation Fans, we got your back," "Great job. Red Sox Nation stands behind you," and "Curt, I know you are telling the truth, and the Nation stands behind you. I, and thousands of others, are more than willing to testify to that under oath" (p. 200).

Social media sites provide accessible channels for fans to enact social support toward athletes and sports figures. As these outlets are largely comprised of sympathetic followers, athletes and sports figures can strategically use these channels to broadcast their rationale for their actions and decisions. In doing so, public support is generated and may assist athletes in their efforts to obtain favorable outcomes (e.g., press coverage, contractual terms). For example, an athlete who is holding out for a new contract and is being negatively framed by sports reporters and the sports organization for these actions could employ social media to counter these labels. This also would allow the athlete to review commentary from fans to gauge public support for their position.

Whether sports organizations would be influenced by social media support remains to be seen. However, social media does allow athletes to quickly rally fans to their cause and in some cases, prompt fans to advocate on their behalf. Moreover, social media allows athletes and sports figures to outsource defense to fans as they monitor criticism and censure detractors. In doing so, communicative norms emerge on these sites that equate participation with favorable commentary. This behavior can be further reinforced by athletes publicly thanking those who combat detractors, an acknowledgement that reinforces fan identity and heightens the likelihood for this behavior to continue. Additionally, just as John Daly asked fans to contact and voice their displeasure to Gary Smits, athletes and sports figures could encourage fans to flood sports organization's telephones and e-mail accounts with supportive messages. Athletes and sports figures who use social media to elicit support may want to invoke collective terminology (as Daly did) such as "we" to generate action.

Although social media facilitates prosocial outcomes with fan–athlete communication, fans can quickly turn against athletes and use social media to distribute their contempt. For example, although much of this chapter described the positivity and support that fans offered to Landis, Landis eventually acknowledged that he used performance enhancing drugs for most of his cycling career—including the 2006 TdF (Ford, 2010). This revelation presumably affected fans, particularly those who passionately defended him. This turning point offers some interesting questions that are ripe for scholars to address. For instance, do some fans still support Landis? Does this betrayal prompt antisocial displays towards Landis? Interestingly, the Floydlandis.com site is currently disabled, so for the present time, fans may turn to other social media sites to voice their reactions. Facebook has become a popular venue for some fans and groups such as "F*ck You, Floyd Landis," "Floyd Landis is an idiot," Floyd Landis Sucks," and "We Hate Floyd Landis" have been launched.

Conversely, social media offers fan forums to reconcile with athletes. One of the most noteworthy sports stories that emerged over the past decade involved the proliferation of performance-enhancing drugs in the MLB. Many players initially proclaimed their innocence, only to later acknowledge that they did use these substances. These belated admissions are often couched in a public apology that requests forgiveness from fans. Although fans may initially be offended by this reversal, they may eventually be ready to extend forgiveness, a step that is easily communicated via social media. Consider Mark McGwire, one of the most prominent players to admit to using performance-enhancing drugs after consistent silence about this subject. In 1994, a work stoppage occurred that led to the cancellation of the World Series, and MLB suffered deteriorating popularity. In 1998, McGwire, along with Sammy Sosa, broke Roger Maris' single-season home run record and were largely credited with restoring baseball's popularity (Butterworth, 2007). Several years later, McGwire began to be linked to performance-enhancing drug use but never offered any commentary when inquiries were made. McGwire finally broke his silence on January 11, 2010, when he publicly admitted that he used steroids (ESPN.com, 2010a). Although some fans still might be unwilling to forgive McGwire, others used social media to proclaim their willingness to move on from this transgression. On Facebook, for example, these sentiments can be shared in groups such as "We Forgive You Mark McGwire."

Social media provides athletes and sports figures with strategic tools to generate fan support. Encouraging fans to legitimize their behavior may prompt fans to take tangible action (such as contacting unsympathetic sports journalists), steps that are perhaps an extension of identification. Through social media, fans' dedication can be directly transmitted to athletes and sports figures, further bolstering advocacy efforts on behalf of these individuals. Social media also enables fans to patrol digital forums where they can directly attack athletes' and sports figures' detractors. In doing so, they defend and protect the reputations of athletes and sports figures, public relations efforts that are essentially performed *pro bono*. The future certainly will reveal additional outcomes that will be important for scholars and practitioners to follow. For instance, will more athletes and sports figures voice their displeasure with sports journalists and solicit fans to engage offending reporters? Will social media sites become prevalent tools for athletes to pressure sports organizations to defer to their requests (e.g., contract, trade)? Moreover, when an athlete or sports figure commits a transgression, how do fans respond? And at what point, if at all, is forgiveness extended?

Social media will continue to expand interaction possibilities between fans and athletes and other sports figures. For instance, during the 2010 regular season, NBA player Reggie Evans was voted as the league's dirtiest player by his colleagues. How did Evans learn about this dubious distinction? A fan notified him on Twitter (Ganter, 2010). Such an event would have been nearly impossible only a few short years ago, yet social media enables fans to instantly and conveniently send messages to athletes and sports figures. The immense fan followings present on many athletes' and sports figures' social media sites along with the commentary dispensed therein indicates that fans are diligently using these communicative tools to increase their immediacy with them.

Accordingly, PSI expressed via social media channels will elevate. PSI research sheds light on processes that may account for the increasing propensity to enact PSI using social media. Some people become so involved in programming that they mentally transport themselves into media narratives (Dal Cin, Zanna, & Fong, 2004; Green & Brock, 2000). Additionally, PSI may be predicated on the need to belong and possessing strong attachments toward media figures (J. Cohen, 2004; Cole & Leets, 1999; Greenwood & Long, 2009). Scholars have further posited that PSI and transporting oneself into media narratives are related conceptually (Green, Brock, & Kaufman, 2004; Greenwood, 2008). For sports fans, social media greatly enhances the ability to interject themselves into the media narratives of athletes and sports figures. Fans intervene by encouraging or dissuading athletes and sports figures from making certain decisions, expressing admiration and support, and defending these individuals against their detractors. This behavior is particularly emboldened when athletes and sports figures use social media to solicit information from fans and encourage them to act on their behalf.

Social media also becomes a valuable mechanism for people to display PSI to athletes and sports figures who are no longer active or who have passed away. Social media enables fans to contribute to these individuals' public legacies. For example, Ferriter (2009) explored fan narratives posted on retired NFL players' *Wikipedia* pages. Results indicated that fans used these digital spaces to (a) collectively celebrate and debate the athletes' achievements; and to (b) construct representations of these athletes that promoted future interaction with other participants. Although such opportunities have not been entirely unavailable to fans, social media provides an expansive sphere wherein they can construct and distribute preferred representations, images that may counter mass media framing and public memory. Thus, in using social media to promote ideal legacies of athletes and sports figures, fans intervene in public memory narratives, perhaps feeling "called on" to guard these legacies.

These examples represent only a few of the exciting changes that social media has introduced. Social media has ushered in a fascinating era wherein fans, athletes, and sports figures become digitally connected even as physical barriers between these groups grow larger. Social media's presence in sports seems likely to expand, and therefore, sports organizations, athletes, and fans face an evolving communicative landscape that suggests the need for diligent attention. How each of these groups respond and adapt to changes created by social media will be important. Will athletes increasingly use these forums to encourage fans to advocate on their behalf? Will confrontations between athletes and fans via social media become more prevalent? And, as some athletes are employing social media to post their physical whereabouts, what risks accompany such disclosures? The answers to these and many more questions eagerly await scholars and practitioners.

5

FINAL THOUGHTS

The preceding chapters have offered a glimpse into some of the ways that social media is transforming sports. Accompanying these changes are a host of implications, challenges, and benefits facing sports organizations and athletes. It is worth noting that social media has brought these immense changes in a very short period of time. Indeed, it is only within the past 5 years that social media tools have become significant "players" in the sports world. Social media is not a passing fad, and will only strengthen its impact on the sports world. The capabilities these tools offer athletes, sports organizations, and fans seem too beneficial to expect a complete cessation. Social media platforms will change over time, but the communicative implications will remain, joined by others as these technologies continue to advance. Thus, sports organizations and athletes should consider a proactive approach in monitoring social media trends and managing their capabilities. In this concluding chapter, I summarize some potentialities for social media and offer suggestions on ways that sports organizations, athletes, and other stakeholders can work in concert to manage these tools.

First, one of the more compelling trends that social media has produced is giving athletes broadcasting channels to break news and contest media framing. Social media empower athletes to literally transmit anything they feel worth sharing. Although this ability presents many advantages, it brings with it the potential for misstep. We may never see another athlete blog his or her retirement, yet more athletes are using social media to announce their playing destinations. To that end, social media soon may become the default venue for this news to be released. Furthermore, considering that many social media sites allow users to seamlessly integrate video and audio tools in their messages, athletes may start constructing their own press conferences that are then broadcast directly to fans. In doing so, a press conference may involve questions asked by fans via Twitter instead of inquires emanating from reporters. Sports organizations and sports reporters would presumably desire to be involved in the production of these events, but athletes may heighten their control over presentation format.

Not every athlete possesses the status and bargaining power to negotiate these events, but elite athletes certainly do and also could supplement these events by selling advertising. NBA superstar LeBron James offered a glimpse of this potential during his free agency that culminated in "The Decision." James announced his playing destination from a Connecticut Boys & Girls Club, securing ESPN to broadcast the event. ESPN agreed— although James and his representatives maintained strict control over broadcasting format. They selected the interviewer (Jim Gray) and determined that advertising revenues would be donated to the Boys & Girls Club. James also announced that via Twitter, fans could send him questions about his decision, which generated voluminous responses. Both James and ESPN received considerable criticism for this event, but nevertheless, it provides a very illuminating glimpse of the future.

Moreover, as athletes and sports figures maintain considerable control over social media messages, these channels may be optimal venues to enact image repair. Baltimore Ravens wide receiver Donte Stallworth is a notable example of this concept. On March 14, 2009, Stallworth, then playing for the Cleveland Browns, hit and killed a pedestrian in Miami, Florida (Wood, 2009). Stallworth pleaded guilty and spent 24 days in jail, and was suspended for the 2009-2010 season by NFL commissioner Roger Goodell (Battista, 2009a). After being reinstated in February 2010, Stallworth was released by the Browns, and subsequently signed with the Ravens (Jensen, 2010). Although Stallworth has publicly expressed his appreciation for another chance to play in the NFL (Bell, 2010), he also has supplemented these pronouncements by using Twitter. Examples include:

> "Everyone have a great night. ... Remember to count your blessings bc we are all blessed in our own unique way. ... Good night & God bless." (June 8, 2010)

"Goodnight & God bless you all. ... Sleep well & wake up in the morning with a positive attitude. ... It'll carry you throughout the day." (June 3, 2010)

"All changes have their melancholy; for what we leave behind us is a part of ourselves; we must die to one life before we can enter another." (May 30, 2010)

In transmitting these messages to his Twitter followers, Stallworth communicated outward evidence of an inward change, inspiration that potentially prompts readers to identify with him. Whereas critical press coverage of Stallworth was perhaps a natural consequence of his actions, social media offered him a space to distribute positivity. Such capability may significantly enhance an athlete's ability to rebuild their public image and facilitate support from fans as they move forward. This does not suggest that athletes should be spared from any consequences, only that social media is a strategic tool that enables them to publicize their efforts to mitigate wrongdoing. This also may be crucial as an athlete's public image is a significant driver to obtaining endorsements. Thus, when their public profile is damaged, social media becomes a conduit for them to enact image repair in a visible forum where both fans and potential sponsors can witness their rehabilitation. Additionally, supportive fan commentary posted on social media sites may influence sponsors as they have evidence that fans are behind the athlete. Although detractors may appear, supportive fans can contend with these critics and drive them from the forum.

This book has discussed several challenges that social media creates for sports organizations and athletes and suggests that these issues should be managed collectively. In doing so, social media messages that create public relations issues may decrease and conflict between athletes and sports organizations may be reduced. One issue that seems important to address is the broadcasting of physical whereabouts. Although social media is a fun way for athletes and sports figures to connect with fans, these disclosures may bring unnecessary risks. Indeed, research suggests that some fans are willing to engage in hostile acts toward opposing teams and players to ensure their team succeeds (Wann et al., 2005). Thus, when athletes publicly disclose their physical location, this may provide maliciously minded individuals ample opportunity to inflict harm.

Additionally, although much of this text has centered on professional sports, collegiate athletic programs may be at more significant risk. For instance, social media gives agents ample opportunity to contact student-athletes, and athletic departments may be unaware this contact is occurring until it is too late. It may be beneficial for student-athletes to receive training including guidance about social media content and allowing potentially harmful people access to their social media profiles. Furthermore, social media provides an invaluable resource for the NCAA to monitor athletic programs (Mandel, 2010). In part, this results from many student-athletes having public profiles, allowing anyone to access their messages. Thus, it may be advisable for student-athletes to fully use their privacy settings and be vigilant with the commentary and photographs they post on the site.

Given the multitude of problematic behaviors that can occur online, athletes and sports figures may unknowingly subject themselves to risk if they are too casual about access. Scholars have observed a phenomenon known as cyberstalking, which is classified by troubling behavior one online user displays towards another online participant. These behaviors include (a) seeking and storing information about the victim in order to harass and threaten them both on- and offline; (b) repeatedly sending unsolicited e-mails and instant messaging the victim; and (c) sabotaging the person by sending spam and computer viruses to them. They also involve (d) signing the victim up for unrequested services and purchasing items in their name; (e) impersonating them in online forums; (f) posting hostile information about them in various online spheres; and (g) posting personal information about the victim online and soliciting others to harass the victim (Burgess & Baker, 2002; Finn, 2004; Sheridan & Grant, 2007; Spitzberg & Hoobler, 2002).

Athletes and sports figures may be visible targets for cyberstalking. Indeed, there have been occasions where fake social media accounts have been set up in the name of an athlete or sports personality. For instance, in May 2009, St. Louis Cardinals manager Tony LaRussa filed a lawsuit against Twitter after an imposter set up an account purporting to be LaRussa. This person began sending messages from LaRussa's Twitter account that mocked his past drunk driving issues and the deaths of two Cardinals pitchers (Associated Press, 2009c). One of the messages included, "Lost 2 out of 3, but we made it out of Chicago without one drunk driving incident or dead pitcher" (Associated Press, 2009c). Twitter and LaRussa ultimately settled the case out of court. However, as a result, Twitter implemented a policy to verify the authenticity of accounts by placing a checkmark and the words "verified" next to the person's name (Katz, 2009). Although social media organizations can take steps to verify the authenticity of those who create accounts, this may not stop every perpetrator. It also does not prevent athletes from giving others access to their accounts.

Another important issue that social media creates is that members of the general public can report athletes' private behavior via these networks. This social media feature presents an interesting dynamic. If a person uses social media to broadcast an athlete's private behavior, this is a free monitoring resource for sports organizations. Audience labor is a tactic that organizations employ to obtain resources from audience members. Under the guise of participation, these individuals willingly provide labor that benefits the organization (Andrejevic, 2008). For example, N. Cohen (2008) chronicled how Facebook used audience labor as its primary growth strategy, by encouraging members to send out e-mail invitations to contacts in their e-mail distribution lists. These messages contained an invitation to join Facebook and become "friends" with the message sender in the Facebook community—a strategy that has contributed to Facebook's exponential growth.

Sports fan are a prime target group for audience labor. This stems from identification, particularly if fans perceive that an athlete's behavior is threatening the team's (and therefore the fan's) success. The Internet enables people to capitalize on their access to athletes and report their activity (and to bolster their reports with video and photographic evidence).

Athletes may already limit their public activity to minimize unwanted attention. However, when they do go into public, they may want to consider that their actions could easily be captured by a cellular phone and subsequently broadcasted via social media. Thus, what athletes believe to be private may suddenly publicly appear on Facebook or another social media site. This is not limited to fans however, this also may occur with other players. On November 2, 2010, Detroit Pistons player Charlie Villanueva tweeted that fellow player Kevin Garnett had made derogatory comments to him during a game. Specifically, "KG called me a cancer patient. I'm pissed because u know how many people died from cancer, and he's tossing it like it's a joke." Then on November 3, 2010, he tweeted, "I wouldn't even trip about that, but a cancer patient, I know way 2 many people who passed away from it, and I have a special place for those." Garnett was subsequently bombarded with media attention and denied that he had called Villanueva a cancer patient, but admitted he did tell him that he was a cancer to his team and the NBA.

This incident generated significant discussion about the public/private issues that social media create. Certainly, "trash talking" has been a historical practice in many sports, but professional athletes have rarely publicized this content. Whether athletes curb their "trash talking" or more players reveal what is said to them via social media will be worth watching.

Given the number and complexity of issues that can result from social media use, sports organizations, players associations, agents, athletic departments, and even high school athletic programs, may wish to consider offering social media training. Although such training may exist, and will not entirely eliminate problematic social media incidents occurring in the future, if structured appropriately and significantly participative, these issues may decrease. Furthermore, if younger athletes become aware of the pitfalls that social media can create, this guidance may shape more strategic social media use in the future. Thus, they may be more prepared as they enter the collegiate and professional ranks, avoiding messages that may affect their eligibility and finances.

It also would be advisable for social media training to be tailored to the needs of each sports organization and their players. Similarly, it may be prudent to understand the communication objectives that players have for social media, rather than being lectured to about their evils. One way to accomplish this would be to survey players about their social media use. Questions could measure activity (e.g., how many messages per day) and content (e.g., subject matter of messages). Additional items could include objectives in using social media (e.g., connecting with fans, circumventing sports journalists, taking more control over news release, connecting with other players), and perceptions of social media (e.g., is it an effective media tool? Does it possess public relations utility? Is it a distraction?). Survey items also could ascertain what information, if any, players perceive is "off limits" for social media. Finally, it may be interesting to ask players who abstain from using social media for the rationale behind their digital reticence.

Once this data is analyzed, players could then be categorized into social media "profiles." These profiles could be classified according to a player's use (e.g., high, moderate, low) along with their desired communication objectives and perceptions of social media's utility. Profiles could then be further classified according to their potential for public relations issues. For example, a player who has low social media activity and views social media as a way to occasionally comment on league news seems less likely to post a controversial message. However, a player who sends multiple social media messages daily and whose messages are consistently centered on political issues, sports journalists' inaccuracies, and organizational critique may present a higher risk.

After obtaining these results, sports organizations could then work with players to draft a social media code of conduct to replace or supplement existing social media policies. These documents may include language recognizing that social media possesses important advantages for players along with providing prohibitions and guidelines to assist players in developing and enhancing strategic media use. Sports organizations also may work with a social media consultant to regularly visit with players about social media use and assist with potential or actual incidents. This is just one possible way that social media training could be structured—there are certainly other options for optimal social media management programs.

Whatever steps are taken, it is important to recognize that social media is here to stay. Formats may change, but outcomes, implications, and consequences will only intensify. Social media has ushered in an amazing, yet complex, era for sports organizations, athletes, and fans. It will be fascinating to observe how social media trends continue to play out. With the public visibility of social media, we have a "front-row seat" to witness the evolution of an integrative, participative, and ever-shifting sports world.

REFERENCES

Afifi, W.A., & Metts, S. (1998). Characteristics and consequences of expectation violations in close relationships. *Journal of Social and Personal Relationships, 15*, 365-392.

Alipour, S. (2010, May 31). Candles, candy, bible, condoms. *ESPN The Magazine*, pp. 96-103.

Anderson, T.L., & Emmers-Sommer, T. M. (2006). Predictors of relationship satisfaction in online romantic relationships. *Communication Studies, 57*, 153-172.

Andrejevic, M. (2008). Watching television without pity: The productivity of online fans. *Television & New Media, 9*, 24-46.

Archibold, R.C. (2010, April 23). Arizona enacts stringent law on immigration. *The New York Times*. Retrieved on April 25, 2010, from http://www.nytimes.com/2010/04/24/us/politics/24immig.html.

Associated Press. (2006, May 8). Seahawks, A&M resolve "12th Man" dispute. Retrieved on March 2, 2010, from http://sports.espn.go.com/nfl/news/story?id=2437992.

Associated Press. (2009a, March 29). Cuban fined $25K for ref complaints. Retrieved on April 13, 2010, from http://sports.espn.go.com/nba/news/story?id=4025741.

Associated Press. (2009b, April 11). NCAA: Fan Facebook site violates rules. Retrieved on January 25, 2010, from http://sports.espn.go.com/ncaa/news/story?id=4060673.

Associated Press (2009c, June 5). La Russa sues Twitter over fake page. Retrieved on November 11, 2009, from http://sports.espn.go.com/mlb/news/story?id=4230602.

Associated Press. (2009d, June 17). Love: McHale won't return. Retrieved on July 7, 2009, from http://sports.espn.go.com/nba/news/story?id=4265512.

Associated Press. (2009e, August 4). Cromartie tweets food, then gets fined. Retrieved on August 30, 2009, from http://sports.espn.go.com/nfl/training-camp09/news/story?id=4376876.

Associated Press. (2009f, August 31). League announces policy on social media before and after games. Retrieved on February 18, 2010, from http://www.nfl.com/news/story?id=09000d5d8124976d&template=without-video-with-comments&confirm=true.

Associated Press. (2009g, September 28). No twitter use for Tech players. Retrieved on April 22, 2010, from http://sports.espn.go.com/ncf/news/story?id=4511880.

Associated Press. (2010a, January 27). Oden sorry photos have surfaced. Retrieved on February 17, 2010, from http://sports.espn.go.com/nba/news/story?id=4861469.

Associated Press. (2010b, February 9). Hill apologizes for nude photos. Retrieved on February 17, 2010, from http://sports.espn.go.com/nba/news/story?id=4900803.

Associated Press. (2010c, March 23). Canseco: Clemens grand jury subpoenaed me. Retrieved on May 3, 2010, from http://msn.foxsports.com/mlb/story/jose-canseco-roger-clemens-grand-jury-032310.

Associated Press. (2010d, May 21). Employee posts draft "plan" on Facebook. Retrieved on July 23, 2010, from http://sports.espn.go.com/nba/draft2010/news/story?id=5208732

Atton, C. (2009). Why alternative journalism matters. *Journalism, 10,* 283-285.

AZcentral.com. (2010, May 14). Arizona Cardinals' Darnell Dockett stirs controversy with tweet. Retrieved on May 17, 2010, from http://www.azcentral.com/sports/cardinals/articles/2010/05/14/20100514arizona-cardinals-darnell-dockett-tweet-controversy.html.

Bargh, J.A., McKenna, K.Y.A., & Fitzsimons, G.M. (2002). Can you see the real me? Activation and expression of the "true self" on the internet. *Journal of Social Issues, 58,* 33-48.

Battista, J. (2009a, August 14). Goodell suspends Stallworth for the season. *The New York Times.* Retrieved from the Lexis-Nexis Academic Database.

Battista, J. (2009b, November 10). As Johnson's suspension ends, so does his time with the Chiefs. *The New York Times.* Retrieved from the Lexis-Nexis Academic Database.

Bell, J. (2010, April 2). Death weighs on Stallworth. *USA Today.* Retrieved from the Lexis-Nexis Academic Database.

Bickley, D. (2009, September 21). A tweet Cards fans won't enjoy. Retrieved on March 29, 2010, from http://www.azcentral.com/members/Blog/DanBickley/63411.

Bierman, F., & Hoffman, B. (2009, March 22). Off the dribble. *The New York Times.* Retrieved from the Lexis-Nexis Academic Database.

Bishop, G. (2009, October 12). Feely flexes his mind, and his thumbs on Twitter. *The New York Times*. Retrieved from the Lexis-Nexis Academic Database.

Bishop, R. (2005). The wayward child: An ideological analysis of sports contract holdout coverage. *Journalism Studies, 6*, 445-459.

Boyd, J. (2000). Selling home: Corporate stadium names and the destruction of commemoration. *Journal of Applied Communication Research, 28*, 330-346.

Boyle, B.A., & Magnusson, P. (2007). Social identity and brand equity formation: A comparative study of collegiate sports fans. *Journal of Sport Management, 21*, 497-520.

Brewer, K. (2007a, April 30). A bloody good, self-righteous pitcher. *The Washington Times*. Retrieved from the Lexis-Nexis Academic Database.

Brewer, K. (2007b, May 14). Stubborn Schilling stealing spotlight. *The Washington Times*. Retrieved from the Lexis-Nexis Academic Database.

Burgess, A.W., & Baker, T. (2002). Cyberstalking. In J.C.W. Boom & L. Sheridan (Eds.), *Stalking and psychosexual obsession: Psychological perspectives for prevention, policing, and treatment* (pp. 201-219). Chichester, UK: Wiley.

Burgoon, J.K. (1993). Interpersonal expectations, expectancy violations, and emotional communication. *Journal of Language and Social Psychology, 12*, 12-21.

Butler, B., & Sagas, M. (2008). Making room in the lineup: Newspaper web sites face growing competition for sports fans' attentions. *International Journal of Sport Communication, 1*, 17-25.

Butterworth, M.L. (2007). Race in "the race": Mark McGwire, Sammy Sosa, and heroic constructions of whiteness. *Critical Studies in Media Communication, 24*, 228-244.

Carpenter, S. (2008). How online citizen journalism publications and online newspapers utilize the objectivity standard and rely on external sources. *Journalism & Mass Communication Quarterly, 85*, 531-548.

Cialdini, R.B., Borden, R.J., Thorne, A., Walker, M.R., Freeman, S., & Sloan, L.R. (1976). Basking in reflected glory: Three (football) studies. *Journal of Personality and Social Psychology, 34*, 366-375.

Cimini, R. (2009a, May 15). Jets not at all a-Twitter. Upset with tweets from Washington's agent. *The New York Daily News*. Retrieved from the Lexis-Nexis Academic Database.

Cimini, R. (2009b, October 1). Clowney practice also tweets Ryan. *The New York Daily News*. Retrieved from the Lexis-Nexis Academic Database.

Cimini, R. (2010, March 5). Gang green gets charged up. Make deal for iffy CB Cromartie. *New York Daily News*. Retrieved from the Lexis-Nexis Academic Database.

Clarridge, E. (2007, September 30). Pray Ball! Is it ok to ask God for a Met miracle? *New York Newsday*. Retrieved from the Lexis-Nexis Academic Database.

Clavio, G. (2009). Interview with Will Leitch, founding editor of Deadspin. *International Journal of Sport Communication, 2*, 293-296.

Cohen, J. (2004). Parasocial break-up from favorite television characters: The role of attachment styles and relationship intensity. *Journal of Social and Personal Relationships, 21*, 187-202.

Cohen, N. S. (2008). The valorization of surveillance: Towards a political economy of Facebook. *Democratic Communiqué, 22*, 5-22.

Cohn, B. (2004, January 3). Favre still working his magic; Quarterback shines in wake of his father's death. *The Washington Times.* Retrieved from the Lexis-Nexis Academic Database.

Cole, T., & Leets, L. (1999). Attachment styles and intimate television viewing: Insecurely forming relationships in a parasocial way. *Journal of Social and Personal Relationships, 16,* 495-511.

Connolly, D. (2007, April 27). Suddenly on the spot, Thorne regrets Schilling comment: Broadcaster regrets "honest mistake." *The Baltimore Sun.* Retrieved from the Lexis-Nexis Academic Database.

Corazza, R. (2010, January 6). Arenas spills his side on Twitter. Retrieved on June 9, 2010, from http://sports.espn.go.com/espn/thelife/news/story?id=4798769.

Cromwell, G. (2009, August 26). Armstrong's tweet turns out more than 1,000 riders for a jaunt around Dublin. Retrieved on September 3, 2010, from http://velonews.com/article/97144/armstrong-s-tweet-turns-out-more-than-1000-riders-.

Cuaycong, A. (2002, January 10). Courtside: A Cuban supporter in me. *BusinessWorld.* Retrieved on September 28, 2007, from the Lexis-Nexis Academic Database.

Dal Cin, S., Zanna, M.P., & Fong, G.T. (2004). Narrative persuasion and overcoming resistance. In E.S. Knowles & J.A. Linn (Eds.), *Resistance and persuasion* (pp. 175-191). Mahwah, NJ: Erlbaum.

Darnell, M.J. (2009, July 30). Visanthe Shiancoe does not find team meetings entertaining. Retrieved on January 8, 2010, from http://sports.yahoo.com/nfl/blog/shutdown_corner/post/Visanthe-Shiancoe-does-not-find-team-meetings-en?urn=nfl,179889.

Davis, N. (2010, March 4). Market about to be flooded; once midnight ET strikes, deals can, too. *USA Today.* Retrieved from the Lexis-Nexis Academic Database.

Debatin, B., Lovejoy, J.P., Horn, A. K., & Hughes, B.N. (2009). Facebook and online privacy: Attitudes, behaviors, and unintended consequences. *Journal of Computer-Mediated Communication, 15,* 83-108.

Deuze, M. (2006). Participation, remediation, bricolage: Considering principal components of a digital culture. *The Information Society, 22,* 63-75.

Dominick, J.R. (1999). Who do you think you are? Personal home pages and self-presentation on the world wide web. *Journalism & Mass Communication Quarterly, 76,* 646-658.

Edes, G. (2007, April 26). Bloody mess—Schilling's sock called into question. *The Boston Globe.* Retrieved on January 24, 2008, from the Lexis-Nexis Academic Database.

Elfin, D. (2009, December 31). This is goodbye ... for now. *The Washington Times.* Retrieved on January 10, 2010, from http://www.washingtontimes.com/weblogs/redskins/2009/dec/31/this-is-goodbye-for-now.

Elzweig, B., & Peeples, D. K. (2009). Using social networking web sites in hiring and retention decisions. *S.A.M. Advanced Management Journal, 74,* 27-36.

ESPN.com. (2009a, April 4). Dawkins giving ex-Eagles worker tickets. Retrieved on April 11, 2009, from http://sports.espn.go.com/nfl/news/story?id=4041720.

ESPN.com. (2009b, September 22). Redskins rookie sorry for Twitter post. Retrieved on September 30, 2009, from http://sports.espn.go.com/nfl/news/story?id=4492151.

ESPN.com. (2009c, September 29). Johnson suffers extensive neck injuries. Retrieved on October 17, 2009, from http://sports.espn.go.com/ncf/news/story?id=4512778.

ESPN.com. (2010a, January 12). McGwire apologizes to La Russa, Selig. Retrieved on February 21, 2010, from http://sports.espn.go.com/mlb/news/story?id=4816607.

ESPN.com. (2010b, May 25). Bowe's story has Chiefs in lockdown. Retrieved on May 28, 2010, from http://sports.espn.go.com/nfl/news/story?id=5215513.

ESPN.com. (2010c, July 11). 6PM ET: Ratings for the "Decision" revealed, Josh Beckett throws 4 innings of rehab ball, Justin Verlander & Andrew Bailey are all-stars. Retrieved on July 12, 2010, from http://espn.go.com/blog/sportscenter/post/_/id/65612/6pm-et-ratings-for-lebrons-decision-revealedjosh-beckett-throws-4-innings-of-rehab-ball-justin-verlander-and-andrew-bailey-join-al-roster

Facebook.com. (2010). Retrieved on July 30, 2010, from http://www.facebook.com/press/info.php?statistics.

Ferriter, M.M. (2009). "Arguably the greatest": Sports fans and communities at work on Wikipedia. *Sociology of Sport Journal, 26*, 127-154.

Fink, J.S., Parker, H.M., Brett, M., & Higgins, J. (2009). Off-field behavior of athletes and team identification: Using social identity theory and balance theory to explain fan reactions. *Journal of Sport Management, 23*, 142-155.

Finn, J. (2004). A survey of on-line harassment at a university campus. *Journal of Interpersonal Violence, 19*, 468-483.

Fisher, R.J. (1998). Group-derived consumption: The role of similarity and team attractiveness in identification with a favorite sports team. *Advances in Consumer Research, 25*, 283-288.

Flanagin, A.J., & Metzger, M.J. (2000). Perceptions of internet information credibility. *Journalism & Mass Communication Quarterly, 77*(3), 515-540.

Flew, T., & Wilson, J. (2010). Journalism as social networking: The Australian youdecide project and the 2007 federal election. *Journalism, 11*, 131-147.

Florio, M. (2010, May 19). Dwayne Bowe lets a rather large cat out of the bag. Retrieved on May 27, 2010, from http://profootballtalk.nbcsports.com/2010/05/19/dwayne-bowe-lets-a-rather-large-cat-out-of-the-bag/.

Ford, B.D. (2010, May 21). Landis admits doping, accuses Lance. Retrieved on July 1, 2010, from http://sports.espn.go.com/mlb/news/story?id=4816607.

FoxSports.com. (2009, December 20). Bucks rookie Jennings fined $7,500 for Tweet. Retrieved on December 29, 2009, from http://msn.foxsports.com/nba/story/Bucks-Jennings-Twitter-fine-121809.

Fraser, B.P., & Brown, W.J. (2002). Media, celebrities, and social influence: Identification with Elvis Presley. *Mass Communication & Society, 5*, 183-206.

Ganter, M. (2010, March 4). Raps' Evans gets down and dirty; known league-wide as dispenser of tough love. *The Toronto Sun*. Retrieved from the Lexis-Nexis Academic Database.

Gantz, W., Wang, Z., Paul, B., & Potter, R.F. (2006). Sports versus all comers: Comparing TV sports fans with fans of other programming genres. *Journal of Broadcasting and Electronic Media, 50*, 95-118.

Genova, G.L. (2009). No place to play: Current employee privacy rights in social networking sites. *Business Communication Quarterly, 72*, 97-101.

Gibbs, J.L., Ellison, N.B., & Heino, R.D. (2006). Self-presentation in online person-als: The role of anticipated future interaction, self-disclosure, and perceived success in Internet dating. *Communication Research, 33*, 152-177.

Giles, D.C. (2002). Parasocial interaction: A review of the literature and a model for future research. *Media Psychology, 4*, 279-305.

Gleich, U. (1997). Parasocial interaction with people on the screen. In P. Winterhoff-Spurk & T. H. A. Van der Voort (Eds.), *New horizons in media psychology: Research co-operation and projects in Europe* (pp. 35-55). Opladen, Germany: Westduetscher Verlag.

Gola, H. (2010, March 4). Daly's tweet revenge. In snit, puts writer's cell number on the web. *New York Daily News*. Retrieved from the Lexis-Nexis Academic Database.

Goldsmith, D. (2004). *Communicating social support*. Cambridge, UK: Cambridge University Press.

Gonzalez, J. (2010, March 12). Gonzo: Shawn Andrews' tweets: Follow if you can. *The Philadelphia Inquirer*. Retrieved from the Lexis-Nexis Academic Database.

Green, M.C., & Brock, T.C. (2000). The role of transportation in the persuasiveness of public narratives. *Journal of Personality and Social Psychology, 79*, 701-721.

Green, M.C., Brock, T.C., & Kaufman, G.F. (2004). Understanding media enjoy-ment: The role of transportation into narrative worlds. *Communication Theory, 14*, 311-327.

Greenwood, D.N. (2008). Television as escape from self: Psychological predictors of media involvement. *Personality and Individual Differences, 44*, 414-424.

Greenwood, D.N., & Long, C.R. (2009). Psychological predictors of media involve-ment: Solitude experiences and the need to belong. *Communication Research, 36*, 637-654.

Gregory, S. (2009, October 26). Did Deadspin hit ESPN below the belt? Retrieved on November 8, 2009, from http://www.time.com/time/business/arti-cle/0,8599,1932286,00.html.

Gullan, S. (2009, August 17). Lewis under fire for latest rant. *The Daily Telegraph* (Australia). Retrieved from the Lexis-Nexis Academic Database.

Hamdy, N. (2009). Arab citizen journalism in action: Challenging mainstream media, authorities and media laws. *Westminster Papers in Communication & Culture, 6*, 92-112.

Hickman, N. (2009, September 12). Tweet smell of success for Bent. *The Express*. Retrieved from the Lexis-Nexis Academic Database.

Hirt, E.R., Zilmann, D., Erickson, G.A., & Kennedy, C. (1992). Costs and benefits of allegiance: Changes in fans' self-ascribed competencies after team victory versus defeat. *Journal of Personality and Social Psychology, 63*, 724-738.

Hlebec, V., Manfreda, K.L., & Vehovar, V. (2006). The social support networks of internet users. *New Media & Society, 8*, 9-32.

Hogg, M.A., & Abrams, D. (1999). Social identity and social cognition: Historical background and current trends. In D. Abrams & M.A. Hogg (Eds.), *Social identity and social cognition* (pp. 1-25). Malden, MA: Blackwell.

Horton, D., & Wohl, R.R. (1956). Mass communication and para-social interaction. *Psychiatry, 19*, 215-229.

http://deadspin.com.

http://profootballtalk.nbcsports.com/about.

HuffingtonPost.com. (2010, February 21). Elijah Fields' money pictures: Twitter photos followed by dismissal. Retrieved on March 18, 2010, from http://www.huffingtonpost.com/2010/02/21/elijah-fields-money-pictu_n_470953.html.

Hutchins, B., & Rowe, D. (2009). From broadcast scarcity to digital plentitude. *Television & New Media, 10*, 354-370.

Isola, F. (2006, June 21). Its another Cuban crisis. NBA fines Mavs owner 250G. *New York Daily News*. Retrieved from the Lexis-Nexis Academic Database.

Jensen, D. (2010, February 18). Ravens give Stallworth new chance. *St. Petersburg Times* (Florida). Retrieved from the Lexis-Nexis Academic Database.

Jin, B. (2006). Viewing factors in public health entertainment-education programming. *Journal of the Northwest Communication Association, 35*, 79-94.

Johnson, T.J., & Kaye, B.K. (2004). War the blog: How reliance on traditional media and the internet influence credibility perceptions of weblogs among blog users. *Journalism & Mass Communication Quarterly, 81*, 622-642.

Johnson, T. J., Kaye, B. K., Bichard, S. L., & Wong, J. W. (2007). Every blog has its day: Politically-interested internet users' perceptions of blog credibility. *Journal of Computer-Mediated Communication, 13*, 100-122.

Jourdan, K. (2010, June 27). Employer internet monitoring meeting resistance. *The Washington Times*. Retrieved from the Lexis-Nexis Academic Database.

Kassing, J.W. (1997). Articulating, antagonizing, and displacing: A model of employee dissent. *Communication Studies, 48*, 311-332.

Kassing, J.W. (1998). Development and validation of the Organizational Dissent Scale. *Management Communication Quarterly, 12*, 183-229.

Kassing, J.W. (2002). Speaking up: Identifying employees' upward dissent strategies. *Management Communication Quarterly, 16*, 187-209.

Kassing, J.W. (2005). Speaking up competently: A comparison of perceived competence in upward dissent strategies. *Communication Research Reports, 22*, 227-234.

Kassing, J.W. (2007). Going around the boss: Exploring the consequences of circumvention. *Management Communication Quarterly, 21*, 55-74.

Kassing, J.W. (2009a). Breaking the chain of command. *Journal of Business Communication, 46*, 311-334.

Kassing, J.W. (2009b). Editor's introduction. *Electronic Journal of Communication, 19*. Retrieved on October 1, 2009, from http://www.cios.org/www/ ejcmain.htm.

Kassing, J.W., & DiCioccio, R.L. (2004). Testing a workplace experience explanation of displaced dissent. *Communication Reports, 17*, 111-120.

Kassing, J.W., & Sanderson, J. (2009). "You're the kind of guy that we all want for a drinking buddy": Expressions of parasocial interaction on Floydlandis.com. *Western Journal of Communication, 73*, 182-203.

Kassing, J.W., & Sanderson, J. (2010). Tweeting through the Giro: A case study of fan-athlete interaction on Twitter. *International Journal of Sport Communication, 3*, 113-128.

Kassing, J. W., & Sanderson, J. (in press). "Is this a church? Such a big bunch of believers around here!": Fan expressions of social support on Floydlandis.com. *Journal of Communication Studies*.

Katz, L. (2009, June 6). Twitter to roll out "verified accounts" this summer. Retrieved on August 18, 2009, from http://news.cnet.com/8301-1023_3-10258816-93.html.

Kelleher, T. (2009). Conversational voice, communicated commitment, and public relations outcomes in interactive online communication. *Journal of Communication, 59*, 172-188.

Kelleher, T., & Miller, B.M. (2006). Organizational blogs and the human voice: Relational strategies and relational outcomes. *Journal of Computer-Mediated Communication, 11*, 395-414.

Kim, H., & Papacharissi, Z. (2003). Cross-cultural differences in online self-presentation: A content analysis of personal Korean and US home pages. *Asian Journal of Communication, 13*, 100-119.

Kim, J., & Haridakis, P.M. (2009). The role of internet user characteristics and motives in explaining three dimensions of Internet addiction. *Journal of Computer-Mediated Communication, 14*, 988-1015.

Kirkendall, J. (2009, July 17). Shayne Graham supposedly frustrated about team asking he take a discount during negotiations. Retrieved on August 7, 2009, from http://www.cincyjungle.com/2009/7/17/952771/shayne-graham-supposedly.

Knott, T. (2009, June 29). This pick may leave Minnesota out in cold. *The Washington Times.* Retrieved from the Lexis-Nexis Academic Database.

Kriegel, M. (2009a, August 4). On the Mark: Please, not more ocho. Retrieved on August 15, 2009, from http://msn.foxsports.com/nfl/story/9888346/On-the-Mark:-Please,-not-more-Ocho.

Kriegel, M. (2009b, August 25). Web brings us too close to Beasley, others. Retrieved on August 27, 2009, from http://msn.foxsports.com/nba/story/9980116/Web-brings-us-too-close-to-Beasley,-others.

Krizek, B. (2008). Introduction: Communication and the community of sport. *Western Journal of Communication, 72*, 103-106.

Landman, B. (2010, May 4). As Howard fouls mount, so does frustration. *St. Petersburg Times.* Retrieved from the Lexis-Nexis Academic Database.

LaRose, R., Lin, C.A., & Eastin, M.S. (2003). Unregulated internet usage: Addiction, habit, or deficient self-regulation? *Media Psychology, 5*, 225-253.

Lemke, T. (2009). Athletes open up in Twitter arena, short and sweet; fans follow intimacy, inanity of sports stars. *The Washington Times.* Retrieved from the Lexis-Nexis Academic Database.

Lieberman, D. (2009, March 18). Extra! extra! Are newspapers dying? *USA Today.* Retrieved from the Lexis-Nexis Academic Database.

Madden, B. (2007, May 13). Beantown Blabbermouth. In Sox's clubhouse, Curt's loose lips cause big Schill. *New York Daily News.* Retrieved from the Lexis-Nexis Academic Database.

Madrigal, R. (1995). Cognitive and affective determinants of fan satisfaction with sporting event attendance. *Journal of Leisure Research, 27*, 205-227.

Mandel, S. (2010, July 19). NCAA turning up heat on agent-player relations with more probes. Retrieved on July 25, 2010, from http://sports illustrated.cnn.com/2010/writers/stewart_mandel/07/19/ncaa.agents/index.html?eref=sihp.

Mariotti, J. (2004, October 20). Schilling's gut trumps Bambino curse: As gut checks go, you won't see many performances as tough and willful as Schilling's in Game 6. *The Chicago Sun-Times.* Retrieved from the Lexis-Nexis Academic Database.

MacMillan, G. (2010, January 25). Manchester United bans players from using Twitter. Retrieved from the Lexis-Nexis Academic Database.

Maese, R. (2009, August 2). With Twitter's arrival, NFL loses control of image game. *Washington Post.* Retrieved from the Lexis-Nexis Academic Database.

Matz, E. (2010, May 31). Postcards from the edge. *ESPN The Magazine,* pp. 92-95.

McLane, J. (2010, March 18). Eagles release Shawn Andrews. *The Philadelphia Inquirer.* Retrieved from the Lexis-Nexis Academic Database.

McMenamin, D. (2010, May 8). Artest tweets critical of Lakers coach. Retrieved on May 22, 2010, from http://sports.espn.go.com/los-angeles/nba/news story?id=5171852.

Mean, L.J., & Kassing, J.W. (2008). Identities at youth sporting events: A critical discourse analysis. *International Journal of Sport Communication, 1,* 42-66.

Meraz, S. (2009). Is there an elite hold? Traditional media to social media agenda setting influence in blogs networks. *Journal of Computer-Mediated Communication, 14,* 682-707.

Mercurio, E., & Filak, V.F. (2010). Roughing the passer: The framing of black and white quarterbacks prior to the NFL draft. *Howard Journal of Communications, 21,* 56-71.

Miller, A.E. (2009). Revealing and concealing postmarital dating information: Divorced coparents' privacy rule development and boundary coordination processes. *Journal of Family Communication, 9,* 135-149.

Miller, J.R. (2010, March 8). Some players cry foul as sports leagues crack down on social networking. FoxNews.com. Retrieved on February 20, 2010, from http://www.foxnews.com/sports/2010/03/10/twitter-facebook-bounds-growing-number-athletes/.

Miller, T. (2009). Media studies 3.0. *Television & New Media,* 10, 5-6.

Nance, R. (2007, February 17). Magical appearance for Johnson, players, fans; All-star MVP award came after HIV announcement. *USA Today.* Retrieved from the Lexis-Nexis Academic Database.

Newman, M. (2010, June 7). Stage is set for ever evolving draft: Fans can follow live on MLB.com, network, Twitter. Retrieved on July 1, 2010, from http://mlb.mlb.com/news/article.jsp?ymd=20100606&content_id=10897462& vkey=news_mlb&fext=.jsp&c_id=mlb.

Oates, T.P. (2009). New media and the repackaging of NFL fandom. *Sociology of Sport Journal, 26,* 31-49.

Palmer, C., & Thompson, K. (2007). The paradoxes of football spectatorship: On-field and online expressions of social capital among the "grog squad." *Sociology of Sport Journal, 24,* 187-205.

Palmgreen, P., Wenner, L.A., & Rayburn, J.D. II. (1980). Relations between gratifications sought and obtained: A study of television news. *Communication Research, 7,* 161-192.

Pandaram, J. (2009, May 12). Facebook and sexting now part of the problem. *Sydney Morning Herald.* Retrieved from the Lexis-Nexis Academic Database.

Parr, B. (2009, September 17). Chad OchoCinco to fly twitter fans to NFL games. Retrieved on October 11, 2009, from http://mashable.com/2009/09/17/ochocinco-twitter-contest/.

Partridge, J. A., Wann, D. L., & Elison, J. (2010). Understanding college sports fans' experiences of and attempts to cope with shame. *Journal of Sport Behavior, 33,* 160-175.

Peluchette, J., & Karl, K. (2009). Examining students' intended image on Facebook: "What were they thinking?!" *Journal of Education for Business, 85,* 30-37.

Pena, J., Walther, J.B., & Hancock, J.T. (2007). Effects of geographic distribution on dominance perceptions in computer-mediated groups. *Communication Research, 34,* 313-331.

People.com. (2010, April 30). Lance Armstrong expecting fifth child. Retrieved on June 15, 2010, from http://celebritybabies.people.com/2010/04/30/lance-armstrong-expecting-fifth-child/?xid=rss-topheadlines.

Perry, S.D., & Lee, K.C. (2007). Mobile phone text messaging overuse among developing world university students. *South African Journal for Communication Theory & Research, 33,* 63-79.

Perse, E.M., & Rubin, R.B. (1989). Attribution in social and parasocial relationships. *Communication Research, 16,* 59-77.

Peter, J., & Valkenburg, P.M. (2006). Individual differences in perceptions of Internet communication. *European Journal of Communication, 21,* 213-226.

Petrecca, L. (2010, March 17). Feel like someone's watching? You're right; workers monitored both off and on the job. *USA Today.* Retrieved from the Lexis-Nexis Academic Database.

Petronio, S. (1991). Communication boundary management: A theoretical model of managing disclosure of private information between martial couples. *Communication Theory, 1,* 311-335.

Petronio, S. (2002). *Boundaries of privacy: Dialectics of disclosure.* Albany: State University of New York Press.

PittsburghChannel.com. (2010, June 23). Pirates put punished pierogi back on field. Retrieved on July 11, 2010, from http://www.thepittsburghchannel.com/sports/24004158/detail.html.

Pompey, K. (2010, February 6). 7th-grade quarterback from Delaware commits to USC. *The Philadelphia Inquirer.* Retrieved from the Lexis-Nexis Academic Database.

Qian, H., & Scott, C.R. (2007). Anonymity and self-disclosure on weblogs. *Journal of Computer-Mediated Communication, 12,* 1428-1451.

Reid, I.A. (2010). "The stone of destiny." Team GB curling as a site for contested national discourse. *Sport in Society, 13,* 399-417.

Reynolds, T. (2009, August 25). Beasley reportedly enters rehab. *The Boston Globe.* Retrieved from the Lexis-Nexis Academic Database.

Riley, C. (2010, June 3). Granholm declares Galarraga's gem a perfect game. Retrieved on June 17, 2010, from http://politicalticker.blogs.cnn.com/category/jennifer-granholm/?fbid=JtgErIkMqDR.

Rowe, D. (2004). *Sport, culture and the media: The unruly trinity* (2nd ed.). Maidenhead, UK: Open University Press.

Rowe, D. (2007). Sports journalism: Still the "toy department" of the news media? *Journalism, 8,* 385-405.

Rowe, D., & Gilmour, C. (2009). Global sport: Where Wembley Way meets Bollywood Boulevard. *Journal of Media & Cultural Studies, 23,* 171-182.

Rubin, A.M. (2000). Impact of motivation, attraction, and parasocial interaction on talk radio listening. *Journal of Broadcasting & Electronic Media, 44,* 635-654.

Rubin, A.M., Haridakis, P.M., & Eyal, K. (2003). Viewer aggression and attraction to television talk shows. *Media Psychology, 5,* 331-362.

Rubin, A.M., & Perse, E.M. (1987). Audience activity and soap opera involvement: A uses and effects investigation. *Human Communication Research, 14,* 246-268.

Rubin, A.M., Perse, E.M., & Powell, R.A. (1985). Loneliness, parasocial interaction and local television news viewing. *Human Communication Research, 12,* 155-180.

Rubin, R.B., & McHugh, M. (1987). Development of parasocial interaction relationships. *Journal of Broadcasting and Electronic Media, 31,* 279-292.

Safko, L., & Brake, D.K. (2009). *The social media Bible: Tactics, tools & strategies for business success.* Hoboken, NJ: Wiley.

Salter, M., & Bryden, C. (2009). I can see you: Harassment and stalking on the Internet. *Information & Communications Technology Law, 18,* 99-122.

Sanderson, J. (2008a). The blog is serving its purpose: Self-presentation strategies on 38pitches.com. *Journal of Computer-Mediated Communication, 13,* 912-936.

Sanderson, J. (2008b). Spreading the word: Emphatic interaction displays on BlogMaverick.com. *Journal of Media Psychology: Theories, Methods, and Applications, 20,* 157-168.

Sanderson, J. (2008c). "You are the type of person that children should look up to as a hero": Parasocial interaction on 38pitches.com. *International Journal of Sport Communication, 1,* 337-360.

Sanderson, J. (2009a). Professional athletes' shrinking privacy boundaries: Fans, ICTs, and athlete monitoring. *International Journal of Sport Communication, 2,* 240-256.

Sanderson, J. (2009b). "Thanks for fighting the good fight": Cultivating dissent on Blogmaverick.com. *Southern Communication Journal, 74,* 390-405.

Sanderson, J. (2010). "The nation stands behind you:" Mobilizing social support on 38pitches.com. *Communication Quarterly, 58,* 188-206.

Sandomir, R. (2009, December 23). TMZ spinoff dedicated to sports is expected. *The New York Times.* Retrieved from the Lexis-Nexis Academic Database.

Schad, J. (2009, December 29). Leach suspended after player complaint. Retrieved on January 4, 2010, from http://sports.espn.go.com/ncf/bowls09/news/story?id=4776848.

Schultz, B., & Sheffer, M. L. (2010). An exploratory study of how Twitter is affecting sports journalism. *International Journal of Sports Communication, 3,* 226-239.

Sharp, D. (2009, September 23). Cyberspace trashing, the vile frontier. *USA Today.* Retrieved from the Lexis-Nexis Academic Database.

Sheridan, L.P., & Grant, T. (2007). Is cyberstalking different? *Psychology, Crime, & Law, 13,* 627-640.

SI.com. (2010, May 13). College basketball: UGA's Fox restricts players from Twitter. Retrieved on May 18, 2010, from http://m.si.com/news/tr/ tr/detail/2594038;jsessionid=C16287DBE2DBDC6E979B79B2A A2AD320.cnnsi1

Somers, K. (2010, May 12). Cardinals lineman Deuce Lutui has no leverage in contract dispute. Retrieved on May 16, 2010, from http://www.azcentral.com/sports/heatindex/articles/2010/05/12/20100512arizona-cardinals-deuce-lutui.html#ixzz0p3asY1yV.

Sood, S., & Rogers, E.M. (2000). Dimensions of parasocial interaction by letter-writers to a popular entertainment-education soap opera in India. *Journal of Broadcasting & Electronic Media, 44*, 386-414.

Soukup, C. (2006). Hitching a ride on a star: Celebrity, fandom, and identification with the world wide web. *Southern Communication Journal, 71*, 319-337.

Snyder, J.L., & Cornetto, K.M. (2009). Employee perceptions of e-mail monitoring from a boundary management perspective. *Communication Studies, 60*, 476-492.

Song, F.W. (2010). Theorizing Web 2.0. *Information, Communication & Society, 13*, 249-275.

Soshnick, S. (2006, May 11). Cuban fined for walking onto the court and mouthing off online about ref selection. *The National Post*. Retrieved from the Lexis-Nexis Academic Database.

Spitzberg, B.H., & Hoobler, G. (2002). Cyberstalking and the technologies of interpersonal terrorism. *New Media & Society, 4*, 71-92.

Sports Business Daily. (2009, August 5). Chargers fine heightens dispute around NFL players' Twitter use. Retrieved on November 3, 2009, from http://www.sportsbusinessdaily.com/article/132277

Sprague, R. (2007). Googling job applicants: Incorporating personal information into hiring decisions. *The Labor Lawyer, 23*, 19-40.

Staples, A. (2009, December 17). Florida recruits offer explanations for controversial MySpace photos. Retrieved on January 18, 2010, from http://sportsillustrated.cnn.com/2009/writers/andy_staples/12/17/orr-trail/index.html.

Staples, A. (2010, January 21). Recruits would be wise not to get too personal on Facebook, web. Retrieved on January 25, 2010, from http:// sportsillustrated.cnn.com/2010/writers/andy_staples/01/21/msu.recruits/index.html.

Stein, M. (2009, September 30). NBA social media guidelines out. Retrieved on October 19, 2009, from http://sports.espn.go.com/nba/news/story?id=4520907.

Stradley, S. (2009, August 27). Chad OchoCinco wants you to help him tweet during games. Retrieved on September 20, 2009, from http://nfl.fanhouse.com/2009/08/27/chad-ochocinco-wants-you-to-help-him-tweet-during-games/.

Strauss, S.M., & Falkin, G.P. (2001). Social support systems of women offenders who use drugs: A focus on the mother. *American Journal of Drug & Alcohol Abuse, 27*, 65-87.

Stubbs, D. (2009). Goalie controversy tweets its ugly head: "Walsh's Twitter-fingers clearly were engaged before his brain was in gear." *The Montreal Gazette*. Retrieved from the Lexis-Nexis Academic Database.

Tajfel, H., & Turner, J.C. (1986). Social identity theory of intergroup behavior. In W. Austin & S. Worchel (Eds.), *Psychology of intergroup relations* (2nd ed., pp. 33-47). Chicago: Nelson-Hall.

Taraszow, T., Aristodemou, E., Shitta, G., Laouris, Y., & Arsoy, A. (2010). Disclosure of personal and contact information by young people in social networking sites: An analysis sing Facebook profiles as an example. International *Journal of Media & Cultural Politics, 6*, 81-101.

Tidwell, L.C., & Walther, J.B. (2002). Computer-mediated communication effects on disclosure, impressions, and interpersonal evaluations: Getting to know one another a bit at a time. *Human Communication Research, 28,* 317-348.

Toronto Sun. (2009, September 8). A.I. inks deal with Memphis. Retrieved from the Lexis-Nexis Academic Database.

Trujillo, N., & Krizek, B. (1994). Emotionality in the stands and in the field: Expressing self through baseball. *Journal of Sport & Social Issues, 18,* 303-325.

Tsao, J. (1996). Compensatory media use: An exploration of two paradigms. *Communication Studies, 47,* 89-109.

Turner, J. C. (1982). Towards a cognitive redefinition of the social group. In H. Tajfel (Ed.), *Self, identity, and intergroup relations* (pp. 15-40). Cambridge, UK: Cambridge University Press.

USA Today. (2009, August 4). Chad Ochocinco in battle with media on twitter, calls writer "idiot." Retrieved on August 8, 2009, from http://content.usato-day.com/communities/thehuddle/post/2009/08/68496123/1.

USA Today. (2010, March 17). Employers use myriad ways to monitor employees. Retrieved from the Lexis-Nexis Academic Database.

Van Grove, J. (2009, October, 26). Larry Johnson's Twitter slur targets coach and heckling fan. Retrieved on November 1, 2009, from http://mashable.com/2009/10/26/larry-johnson-twitter/

van Hemert, S. (2010, February 21). Athletes warned against becoming journalists. *Sunday Times* (South Africa). Retrieved from the Lexis-Nexis Academic Database.

Vinton, N. (2010, April 1). Roger Clemens uses Twitter to say "equipment" works fine after News' report on Rocket's virility. *New York Daily News.* Retrieved on April 5, 2010, from http://www.nydailynews.com/sports/baseball/yan-kees/2010/04/01/2010-04-01_rocket_my_equipment_works_just_fine_thanks.html.

Wakefield, K.L. (1995). The pervasive effects of social influence on sporting event attendance. *Journal of Sport and Social Issues, 19,* 335-351.

Wakefield, K.L., & Wann, D.L. (2006). An examination of dysfunctional sports fans: Method of classification and relationships with problem behaviors. *Journal of Leisure Research, 38,* 168-186.

Wall, M. (2005). "Blogs of war": Weblogs as news. *Journalism, 6,* 153-172.

Walther, J.B. (1992). A longitudinal experiment on relational tone in computer-mediated and face to face interaction. *Proceedings of the Hawaii International Conference on System Sciences, 4,* 220-231.

Walther, J.B. (1996). Computer-mediated communication: Impersonal, interpersonal, and hyperpersonal interaction. *Communication Research, 23,* 3-43.

Walther, J.B., & Boyd, S. (2002). Attraction to computer-mediated social support. In C.A. Lin & D. Atkin (Eds.), *Communication technology and society: Audience adoption and uses* (pp. 153-188). Cresskill, NJ: Hampton Press.

Walther, J.B., & Burgoon, J.K. (1992). Relational communication in computer-mediated interaction. *Human Communication Research, 19,* 50-88.

Walther, J.B., Slovacek, C.L., & Tidwell, L.C. (2001). Is a picture worth a thousand words? Photographic images in long-term and short-term computer-mediated communication. *Communication Research, 28,* 105-134.

Wang, Z., Walther, J.B., Pingree, S., & Hawkins, R.P. (2008). Health information, credibility, homophily, and influence via the Internet: Web sites versus discussion groups. *Health Communication, 23,* 358-368.

Wann, D. L. (2006). The causes and consequences of sport team identification. In A.A. Raney & J. Bryant (Eds.), *Handbook of sports and media* (pp. 331-352). Mahwah, NJ: Erlbaum.

Wann, D.L., & Branscombe, N.R. (1993). Sports fans: Measuring degree of identification with the team. *International Journal of Sport Psychology, 24,* 1-17.

Wann, D.L., Culver, Z., Akanda, R., Daglar, M., De Divitiis, C., & Smith, A. (2005). The effects of team identification and game outcome on willingness to consider anonymous acts of hostile aggression. *Journal of Sport Behavior, 28,* 282-294.

Wann, D.L., Royalty, J., & Roberts, A. (2000). The self-presentation of sports fans: Investigating the importance of team identification and self-esteem. *Journal of Sport Behavior, 23,* 198-206.

Wann, D.L., & Waddill, P.J. (2007). Examining reactions to the Dale Earnhardt crash: The importance of identification with NASCAR drivers. *Journal of Sport Behavior, 30,* 94-109.

Wann, D.L., & Zaichkowsky, L. (2009). Sport team identification and belief in team curses: The case of the Boston Red Sox and the curse of the Bambino. *Journal of Sport Behavior, 32,* 489-502.

Weaver, D., McCombs, M., & Shaw, D.L. (2004). Agenda setting research: Issues, attributes, and influences. In L.L. Kaid (Ed.), *Handbook of political communication research* (pp. 257-282). Mahwah, NJ: Erlbaum.

Weiss, D. (2010, February 7). Recruiting stunt raises bigger NCAA concern. *New York Daily News.* Retrieved from the Lexis-Nexis Academic Database.

Wenner, L.A. (2007). Towards a dirty theory of narrative ethics: Prolegomenon on media, sport and commodity value. *International Journal of Media & Cultural Politics, 3,* 111-129.

Whannel, G. (2001). *Media sports stars: Masculinities and moralities.* London: Routledge.

Who is a journalist? (2008). *Journalism Studies, 9,* 117-131.

Withers, T. (2010, July 6). LeBron finally joins Twitter. Associated Press. Retrieved on July 8, 2010, from http://www.washingtonexaminer.com/sports/nba/LeBron-finally-joins-Twitter-97881659.html.

Wilson, J. (2009, August 1). Bent faces fine over Twitter tirade. *The Daily Telegraph* (London). Retrieved from the Lexis-Nexis Academic Database.

Witt, L. (2004). Is public journalism morphing into the public's journalism? *National Civic Review, 93,* 49-57.

Wood, S. (2009, April 2). DUI manslaughter charges filed against Stallworth. *USA Today.* Retrieved from the Lexis-Nexis Academic Database.

Wyshynski, G. (2010, July 22). Eulogy: Hilariously outrageous twitter ramblings of Paul Bissonnette. Retrieved from http://sports.yahoo.com/nhl/blog/puck_daddy/post/Eulogy-Hilariously-outrageous-Twitter-ramblings?urn=nhl-257447.

Young, B. (2010, May 23). Phoenix Suns' Jared Dudley asked fans for help against Los Angeles Lakers. Retrieved on May 25, 2010, from http://

www.azcentral.com/sports/suns/articles/2010/05/23/20100523phoenix-suns-game-3-twitter.html#ixzz0p6Ds8fUP.

Young, C.W. (2005). Online civic participation and political empowerment: Online media and public opinion format in Korea. *Media, Culture & Society, 27,* 925-935.

Zelkovich, C. (2009, April 24). CFL cautions players about Facebook; social net-working site, along with Twitter, can possibly reveal too much information. *The Toronto Star.* Retrieved from the Lexis-Nexis Academic Database.

Zillgitt, J. (2009, April 29). League commissioners keeping up with Twitter. *USA Today.* Retrieved from the Lexis-Nexis Academic Database.

Zillgitt, J., & Colston, C. (2009, November 5). NBA insider. *USA Today.* Retrieved from the Lexis-Nexis Academic Database.

AUTHOR INDEX

SUBJECT INDEX

CPSIA information can be obtained
at www.ICGtesting.com
Printed in the USA
FFOW01n2133270715
15398FF